CAMPAIGN 342

# THE PARAGUAYAN WAR 1864–70

The Triple Alliance at stake in La Plata

**GABRIELE ESPOSITO**

ILLUSTRATED BY GIUSEPPE RAVA

*Series editor Marcus Cowper*

OSPREY PUBLISHING
Bloomsbury Publishing Plc

Kemp House, Chawley Park, Cumnor Hill, Oxford OX2 9PH, UK
29 Earlsfort Terrace, Dublin 2, Ireland
1385 Broadway, 5th Floor, New York, NY 10018, USA
Email: info@ospreypublishing.com
www.ospreypublishing.com

OSPREY is a trademark of Osprey Publishing Ltd

First published in Great Britain in 2019
Transferred to digital print in 2024

A catalogue record for this book is available from the British Library.

Print ISBN: 978 1 4728 3444 7
ePub : 978 1 4728 3443 0
ePDF: 978 1 4728 3441 6
XML: 978 1 4728 3442 3

Maps by www.bounford.com
3D BEVs by The Black Spot
Index by Alan Rutter
Typeset by PDQ Digital Media Solutions, Bungay, UK
Printed and bound in India by Replika Press Private Ltd.

24 25 26 27 28    10 9 8 7 6 5 4 3 2

## Artist's note

Readers may care to note that the original paintings from which the color
plates in this book were prepared are available for private sale. All
reproduction copyright whatsoever is retained by the publishers. For
further information, please visit:

http://www.g-rava.it/

The publishers regret that they can enter into no correspondence upon
this matter.

Osprey Publishing supports the Woodland Trust, the UK's leading woodland
conservation charity.

To find out more about our authors and books visit
**www.ospreypublishing.com**. Here you will find extracts, author
interviews, details of forthcoming events and the option to sign up for
our newsletter.

## Author's acknowledgments

Special thanks are due to the series editors Marcus Cowper and Nikolai
Bogdanovic for supporting the project of this book from its outset. A
further special acknowledgment goes to Giuseppe Rava, for the stunning
color plates that illustrate this title: thanks to his brilliant artistry, the battles
of the Paraguayan War have been brought to life once again. Last but not
least, I wish to express my deep gratitude to the Paraguayan cultural
institutions that helped me in writing the present book –the Museo Paso
de Patria and Museo del ex-Cuartel de Mariscal López—in the persons of
Vicente Garcia and Vicenta Miranda Ojeda (two great researchers, and now
dear friends of mine).

## Note on photographic images

Unless otherwise indicated, all images that appear in this work are in the
public domain.

## Author's dedication

To my parents Maria Rosaria and Benedetto, for their unconditional love
and great support throughout my life. This book is also dedicated to the
memory of all the brave soldiers who died fighting for their countries
during the Paraguayan War of 1864–70.

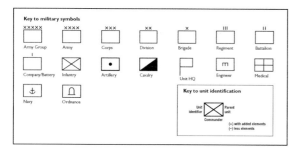

**PREVIOUS PAGE**
The Battle of the Riachuelo.

# CONTENTS

ORIGINS OF THE CAMPAIGN    4
The strategic context

CHRONOLOGY    16

OPPOSING COMMANDERS    19
Paraguayan . Triple Alliance

OPPOSING FORCES    25
Paraguayan . Triple Alliance . The opposing navies

OPPOSING PLANS    34
Paraguayan . Triple Alliance

THE CAMPAIGN    36
Brazil intervenes in Uruguay, 1864 . Paraguay invades Mato Grosso . The Paraguayan occupation of
Corrientes, 1865 . The Battle of the Riachuelo, June 11, 1865 . Yatay and Uruguayana, August–
September, 1865 . The Alliance advance on Paraguay, 1866 . The Battle of Estero Bellaco, May 2, 1866
The First Battle of Tuyutí, May 24, 1866 . The Battle of Boquerón del Sauce, July 1866 . The battles of
Curuzú and Curupaytí, September 1866 . The long stalemate, September 1866–July 1867 . The
Second Battle of Tuyutí, and the fall of Humaitá . The Pikysyry maneuver and the beginning of the
*Dezembrada*, 1868 . The battles of Avay and Lomas Valentinas . The Hills Campaign and the death of
López, 1869–70

AFTERMATH    89

THE BATTLEFIELD TODAY    92

BIBLIOGRAPHY AND FURTHER READING    94

INDEX    95

# ORIGINS OF THE CAMPAIGN

The Paraguayan War, also known as the War of the Triple Alliance, was the greatest and most important military conflict in the history of South America after the Wars of Independence that freed that continent from Spanish and Portuguese colonial rule. It involved four countries and lasted for more than five years, during which Paraguay fought alone against a powerful alliance formed by Brazil, Argentina, and Uruguay (i.e. the Triple Alliance, which gave the war its alternative name).

This conflict was unique in South American military history for a series of reasons, but primarily because of the large number of troops involved and for its terrible cost in lives. It was the only true continental war in South America, which saw a full mobilization of the countries involved in the fighting. The Triple Alliance War cost Brazil 50,000 casualties, Argentina 30,000, and Uruguay 5,000; but these paled in comparison to Paraguayan losses. The catastrophic human price paid by the latter amounted to more than 300,000 lives, some 70 percent of that country's total population. Other related statistics are equally impressive: in the most important pitched battle of the conflict, fought at Tuyutí on May 24, 1866, an army of 32,000 Alliance soldiers defeated a Paraguayan army that numbered around 24,000 men. The Battle of the Riachuelo, fought on the Paraná River on June 11, 1865, was without doubt the largest and most important naval battle ever fought between South American navies. No other war in South America was fought on such a massive scale until the Chaco War of 1932–35 between Bolivia and Paraguay.

From a military history standpoint, the War of the Triple Alliance marked a revolution for the armies of South America. It was the first truly modern conflict on the continent, and took place in a period during which warfare was undergoing radical changes around the world. The innovations that the Europeans and North Americans introduced during conflicts such as the Crimean War, the Austro-Prussian War, and American Civil War were more or less the same as those introduced by Paraguay, Brazil, Argentina, and Uruguay between 1864 and 1870. It is interesting to note how during the years 1860–70, the whole of the Americas was ravaged by war: in the USA, Unionists fought Confederates; in Mexico, Emperor Maximilian I with his European allies was at war with the Republicans of Benito Juárez; and in the Andean region of South America, an alliance formed by Peru, Chile, Ecuador, and Bolivia fought against Spain in the Chincha Islands War.

When the Triple Alliance War broke out in 1864, South American armies were relatively small and lacked professionalism. Their soldiers were poorly

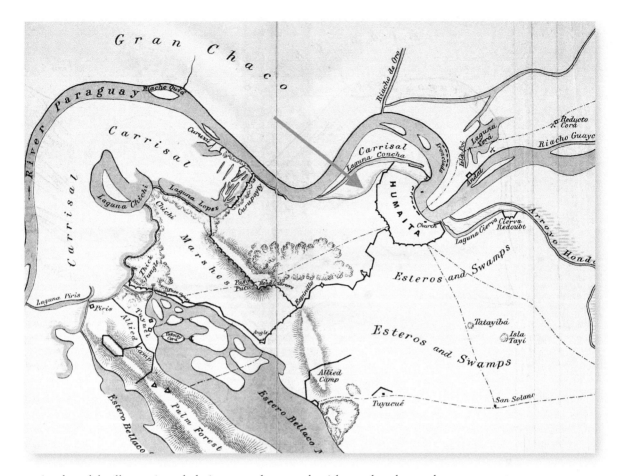

A map showing the location of the Fortress of Humaitá. Between August and October 1867, the Alliance maneuvered to isolate the fortress and cut its lines of supply from Asunción. On February 19, 1868, the Brazilian fleet was finally able to force its way upriver on the Paraguay, bombarding the fortress.

trained and badly equipped, being mostly armed with outdated, surplus weapons from Europe. They were semi-professional forces at best, frequently hated by the populations upon whom they preyed. The endemic political instability within the continental countries had transformed them into instruments of the various *caudillos* (dictators), who very often used them as private armies. The innovations introduced and harsh lessons learned during the Paraguayan War would change all this, in a definitive way. Every new technology available at the time was utilized, including railways to transport troops, telegraphy for communications, and air balloons for reconnaissance purposes.

The greatest revolution took place in the field of weaponry. When the war started, most South American troops were still armed with old flintlock or percussion smoothbore muskets; by the time it ended, most armies had adopted percussion rifles employing the Minié system. New weapons such as breech-loading rifles and Gatling machine guns were tested for the first time, while rifled artillery showed its superiority on the field of battle (in 1867, Argentina was the first South American country to adopt the Krupp artillery system). Such technological improvements also affected naval warfare, with steam-powered and ironclad vessels becoming dominant and with torpedoes being used for the first time in an effective way. The new weapons changed the traditional tactics employed by South American armies profoundly: cavalry, which had always been the most important element on the battlefield, had to abandon the practice of frontal charges, transforming itself for a new mounted-infantry role. As a result, infantry and technical corps (especially engineers) became much more important than before. During the Paraguayan War, military experts with appropriate knowledge were brought in from Europe and the USA by both belligerent sides, starting a general trend that would continue in the following years. Between 1875 and 1910, all South American countries invited foreign military missions to train and organize their forces, with the first response to the new need for professionalism emerging from the Paraguayan War.

The enormous distances involved during the war meant that the conflict was initially a matter of small columns (numbering a few thousand men) marching along the routes of the major rivers and seeking each other out in sparsely inhabited and inhospitable terrain. Paraguay is divided into two main regions by the river that gives the country its name: the western part, known as the Chaco, saw no major military operations. All the battles were fought in the eastern half of the country, located between the rivers Paraguay and Paraná. This area has a very humid subtropical climate, with many small rivers running through swampy jungle valleys covered with tropical vegetation. The abundant rainfall throughout the year, especially between March and May, and October and November, created a punishing physical environment that was difficult to endure for the majority of soldiers, who had to live and fight in the marshy lowlands. In this tough environment, diseases like smallpox, cholera, and typhoid wiped out entire units, causing more deaths than any battle. As a result, the sufferings endured by common soldiers were profound: they were supplied with poor and unreliable rations and faced a constant lack of clean water. Officers often neglected their men, while hygienic and medical support were mostly non-existent. Privation, disease, and famine were the usual companions for armies in the field, which were ill-equipped to resist them. From 1865, the armies involved in the war began to grow larger, leading to a gradual transformation in the nature of the military operations: positional battles were fought at points of strategic importance, such as river crossings or at key Paraguayan defensive positions.

# THE STRATEGIC CONTEXT

## *Paraguayan expansionism*

Before the outbreak of the Wars of Independence in South America, Paraguay was part of the Spanish Empire and, more particularly, of the Viceroyalty of the Río de la Plata. With the May Revolution of 1810, Argentina became independent from Spain and began to launch a series of military expeditions aimed at freeing all the territories of the Viceroyalty of La Plata, which also included Uruguay alongside Paraguay and Argentina. After the revolution in Buenos Aires, Paraguay had remained loyal to Spain and to the governor Bernardo de Velasco: as a result, in September 1810, the Argentine general Manuel Belgrano was sent with 1,500 soldiers to occupy Paraguayan territory. Governor de Velasco called upon Paraguay's poorly armed but cavalry-rich militia, and raised 6,000 men to repulse the Argentine invasion. In the campaign that followed, the *Peninsulares* (Spanish) officers and Velasco melted away in the wake of Belgrano's initial success. The Paraguayan militia was left in the hands of its Creole officers, who were able

# Paraguay before the war

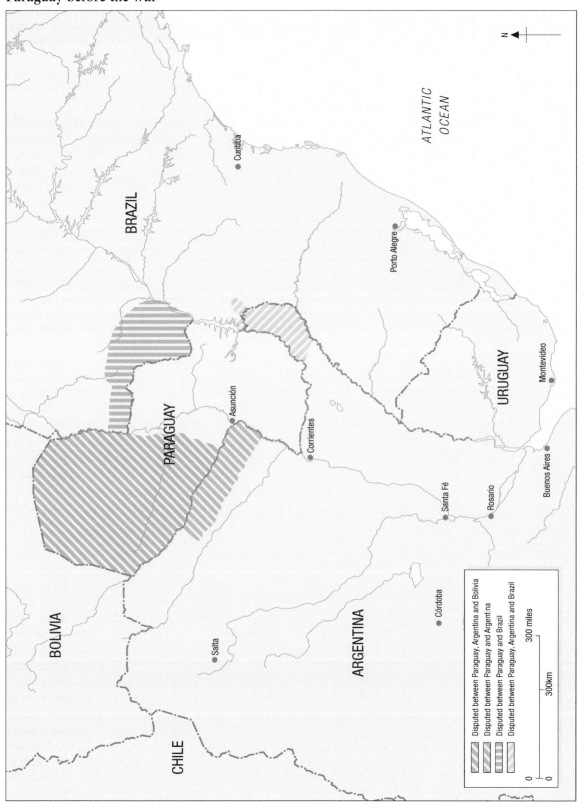

to defeat Belgrano in the subsequent battles of Paraguarí and Tacuarí. As a result of these events, the *Peninsulares* officers were arrested and relieved of command. Governor de Velasco was deposed, and a five-man junta was created. In 1811, Paraguay became an autonomous country, independent from both Spain and Argentina.

For a brief ensuing period, the new nation was ruled by two consuls elected by the National Congress. In 1814, José Gaspar Rodriguez de Francia became dictator of Paraguay. The latter established a salaried army of company-sized units, replacing the old militia system. After heavily purging the existing forces to ensure their loyalty to him, he imposed strict discipline within the ranks. Under his direction, Paraguayan military strength was increased to deter Argentina from further attacks and to act in support of his own autocratic rule. De Francia created a program of conscription and placed landholdings confiscated from his opponents under the control of the army. Because of the blockade by Argentina, great efforts were made to procure, repair, and manufacture weapons: by 1816, guns and cloth for military uniforms were almost entirely produced in Paraguay. The armed forces took 64 percent of the republic's total budget, but soldiers were also employed for public works. Only Francia could appoint officers, who faced instant dismissal if they abused their position.

After de Francia's death, in 1841, the NCOs of the Paraguayan Army mounted a coup and a new National Congress was elected. Don Carlos António López was one of the two consuls elected by the members of the new congress; like de Francia, he soon became the sole ruler of Paraguay thanks to his individual abilities. In 1845, the new dictator completely reorganized and modernized the Paraguayan Army; during that same year, following a treaty with General José María Paz of the Argentine province of Corrientes, some of Paraguay's military forces were sent to assist the Argentine general in his struggle against Juan Manuel de Rosas (at that time dictator of Argentina). Since 1811, Paraguay had not played a significant role in the political and military situation in South America: landlocked, and bordering regional powers like Brazil and Argentina, the small country lacked options to expand its territory. As a result of this situation, de Francia had always preferred to remain neutral during the various conflicts that were fought by bordering countries. The 1845 de Rosas expedition was the first time the Paraguayans sent a military force beyond their national borders, but it ended in total failure. General Paz described the Paraguayan contingent as being in a poor condition: "an unformed mass without instruction, without organization, without discipline, and ignorant of the first rudiments of war." Unsurprisingly, the Paraguayan force ended up retreating without having fought, while its allies were defeated by de Rosas and Paz fled to Paraguay.

After the 1845 disaster, Carlos António López preferred to follow de Francia's example, and abandoned his expansionist ambitions. In the decades that followed, until his death in 1862, the dictator did his best to improve the situation within Paraguay: he recruited foreign specialists, improved communications and infrastructure, sponsored some industrialization, and expanded the military resources of the country. All these measures soon led to a gradual expansion of the Paraguayan population, which was extremely small during de Francia's rule. From a military point of view, Carlos António López adopted several measures with the objective of transforming Paraguay into a country difficult to invade: in the meantime, de Rosas had become supreme ruler of Argentina and had made public on several occasions his intention to annex Paraguay (thus recreating the former Viceroyalty of the Río de la Plata). Fearing a foreign attack from the south, López ordered the construction of the Fortress of Humaitá near the mouth of the Paraguay River: this soon became the most important and impressive military fortification in South America, due to its strategic position.

Thanks to the presence of two massive rivers on Paraguayan territory, the Paraguay and the Paraná, López was able to organize an intelligent system of defence. Paraguay bordered Argentina to the south and to the east, the border being marked in both areas by the Paraná River. In the north, Paraguay bordered Brazil: these regions, however, were mostly uninhabited and covered by impenetrable tropical jungle (in the north lay the Amazonian provinces of Brazil). To the west, Paraguay bordered the desert region of the Chaco: the latter was contested between Argentina and Bolivia, despite being practically impossible to cross by land. Moreover, the immense Paraguay River separated the Chaco from the populated regions of Paraguay. Bearing in mind the geographical and strategic situation described above, López did not fear attack from the north and west; all his efforts were thus aimed at securing dominance over the Paraná River. The Fortress of Humaitá was built at the confluence of the Paraguay River (flowing from the north) and the Paraná River (dividing southern Paraguay from northern Argentina). The confluence between the two rivers was the only point where an invading army could enter Paraguay without major difficulties: with the construction of the new Fortress of Humaitá, completed by 1854, López made his country very difficult to invade. In addition, to control the course of the two great rivers, the Paraguayan dictator ordered the construction of a fleet that would operate on the Paraná and Paraguay, with Humaitá as its main base.

Since the 1840s, Carlos António López had been assisted by his son and future successor Francisco Solano López; the latter had acted as supreme commander of the Paraguayan Army since the expedition to Corrientes in 1845, and had much greater personal ambitions than his father. In 1862, Carlos António López died and his son became the new dictator of Paraguay. The latter had always held a personal fascination with the figure of Napoleon I, and dreamed of emulating his hero by becoming the new absolute military master of the La Plata region. In order to achieve this goal, Francisco Solano López tried to exploit to the full the internal difficulties of his regional rivals. His main objectives were two: obtaining an outlet to the Atlantic Ocean, and occupying new areas rich in natural resources. Paraguay had always suffered from being a landlocked country, especially since the Paraná merges with the Uruguay River at its terminus (forming the River Plate/Río de la Plata, which was controlled by Argentina and Uruguay). Commercial and political relations with the rest of the world were severely damaged by the absence of a Paraguayan port on the Atlantic; as a result, Francisco Solano López had it in mind to conquer Uruguay after intervening in the latter's civil war. Regarding the acquisition of new natural resources, López hoped to occupy the Brazilian provinces of Río Grande do Sul and Mato Grosso. The former had been independent for a decade between 1835 and 1845, rebelling against Brazil during the so-called *Farrapos* (or Ragamuffins) Revolt; as a result, the Paraguayans

The Brazilian Emperor Pedro II (on the left), with his sons-in-law the Duke of Saxe-Coburg-Gotha (center) and the Count of Eu (on the right). They are all dressed in the campaign uniform prescribed for Brazilian generals.

The Duke of Caxias, one of the most important Alliance commanders in the Paraguayan War. When he was given command of Brazilian forces in October 1866, he found the army hungry, disease-ridden, and demoralized after the defeat at Curupaytí. Caxias instituted reforms that fundamentally improved the Brazilian Army's discipline and quality.

thought that Río Grande do Sul would ally with their cause. Río Grande do Sul was extremely rich thanks to the profitable cultivation of yerba, used to make maté—a staple beverage that is extremely popular in the La Plata region. Mato Grosso was full of mineral resources that could help Paraguay to expand its industry and economy. Both territories were located on the borders of Brazil, far from the great centers of the north.

### Brazil: the leading power in South America

In November 1807, Napoleon I invaded Portugal, thus obliging the Portuguese court to abandon Europe in order to avoid capture by the French. The Portuguese royals went to Brazil with most of their military fleet, establishing themselves in South America. As a result, having been a simple colony for centuries, Brazil soon became the center of the Portuguese Empire. In 1815, Brazil was elevated to the rank of kingdom and was formally unified with Portugal as a single state. The presence of the Portuguese royals in Latin America led to the birth of Brazilian expansionism: during the 18th century, Spain and Portugal had already fought each other for possession of some border territories such as Uruguay, and now this struggle would continue, but with different actors.

Soon after gaining its independence, Argentina became the main regional rival of Brazil: Paraguay and Uruguay were the objectives of both contenders, since their borders were not defined with any form of precision. The Argentines helped the Uruguayans in their struggle against Spanish rule, but in 1816, Uruguay was occupied by Portuguese and Brazilian military forces. At this time, the Argentines were still at war with Spain in other areas of South America, and thus could not start a large-scale war against the Kingdom of Portugal and Brazil. As a result, Uruguay remained a province of Brazil for several years.

In 1821, the King of Portugal and Brazil returned to Europe and left his eldest son Pedro in Brazil, who was to act as regent for that part of the kingdom. In 1822, however, Pedro decided to rise up in revolt against his father in order to transform Brazil into an independent country. By that year, most of South America had become independent from Spanish rule and thus the Brazilians hoped to use their global superiority against the newly formed Spanish-speaking republics. During the period when most of South America was under Spanish control, the Portuguese could not expand in that continent without fearing a Spanish invasion of their home country in Europe; now that Spain was out of Latin America, however, this danger had passed. Obviously, Pedro's independence movement was strongly supported by the local dominant classes in Brazil, but it was opposed by the Portuguese and by their military garrisons. In 1822, the troops arriving from Portugal, who remained loyal to the crown, attempted to stop the secession; those recruited locally in Brazil, in contrast, all joined Pedro's cause. By 1823, the independents had liberated most of Brazil, and the Portuguese remained in possession of only a few cities and ports. In 1824, the last of these Portuguese strongholds—the Uruguayan capital of Montevideo—was conquered by the Brazilians, and the following year, the Empire of Brazil formally proclaimed its independence.

The new state inherited all the expansionist ambitions of the previous Portuguese colony, and had to face a series of problems on its borders. The first and most important of these was the question over Uruguay: the Argentines had never abandoned their dream of conquering the "Eastern Bank" of the River Plate, while the Uruguayans hoped to obtain independence from Brazil with the decisive support of Argentina. As a result, just a few months after becoming an autonomous nation, Brazil had to fight the Cisplatine War against the Argentines for possession of Uruguay. The conflict lasted until 1828, and was the largest military confrontation fought to date between the two leading military powers of South America. Military operations ended in complete stalemate, since both sides had serious internal difficulties and were in no condition to defeat the enemy in a decisive manner. According to the Treaty of Montevideo, both Brazil and Argentina renounced their claims on Uruguay, and the latter became an independent republic. During the following decades, however, both Brazil and Argentina continued to exert a strong influence over Uruguay, intervening (directly or indirectly) in the internal politics of the small country. Soon after independence, Uruguay was ravaged by a bitter civil war that continued for several decades across different phases: both Brazil and Argentina lent support to the two opposing parties, thus fighting a proxy war between each other in Uruguay.

Since 1828, Pedro I of Brazil had been involved in Portuguese political struggles concerning the succession to his father's throne. According to the Portuguese Constitutional Charter of 1826, the legitimate heir to the Portuguese throne was Pedro's daughter (since Brazil and Portugal could not be unified again under a single monarch). Pedro's younger brother Miguel, who had remained in Portugal, did not accept this situation and was

A Brazilian volunteer of the Zuavos da Bahia. This unit was formed from free black men from the province of Bahia, who wished to fight for their homeland in order to show that slavery had to be abolished in the empire. (Drawing by Benedetto Esposito; author's collection)

Brazilian volunteer of the 16° Corpo de Voluntários Auxiliar. This unit was formed from volunteers of many nationalities (mostly Italians) living in Uruguay, who were recruited in Montevideo during the Brazilian intervention of 1864. The unit was clearly inspired by Garibaldi's "Red Shirts" and was thus nicknamed the Voluntários Garibaldinos. (Drawing by Benedetto Esposito; author's collection)

crowned King of Portugal with the support of Portuguese conservatives. The Portuguese liberals, instead, supported the legitimate claims of Pedro and of his daughter. A civil war between the conservatives and liberals soon broke out, and the military situation gradually shifted in favor of the former; as a result, in 1831, Pedro opted to abdicate and leave Brazil in order to go to Portugal and personally fight for the rights of his daughter. The Brazilian throne passed to Pedro II, a younger son of Pedro I. Because Pedro II was only six years old in 1831, Brazil entered a period of political instability in the years that followed. From 1835 to 1845, the empire was ravaged by the *Farrapos* Revolt, a civil war that saw the secession of Río Grande do Sul province from the rest of Brazil. The Brazilian authorities faced many difficulties in crushing the revolt, which finally came to an end only after a decade of harsh fighting.

Meanwhile, during those same years, the dictator de Rosas had risen to political prominence in Argentina and was now attempting to exert increasing influence over Uruguay. By 1851, political tension in the River Plate area was ready to explode into full-scale conflict, since Argentina was also now ravaged by a cruel civil war between de Rosas and his internal enemies. At this point, Pedro II, having come of age as a monarch, decided to intervene against de Rosas and his Uruguayan supporters. This marked the beginning of the Platine War, which ended in 1852 with the defeat of de Rosas. The latter was replaced by Justo José de Urquiza, an ally of Brazil who had guided the anti-de Rosas Argentine military forces during the last civil war. In Uruguay, the civil war came to a temporary halt, and the two opposing parties tried to find compromise. The military intervention of Brazil had restored the balance of power in the River Plate region.

This positive outcome, however, did not last for long; with the ascendancy of Francisco Solano López in 1862, Paraguay became a threat to the region's stability. Meanwhile, the political compromise that had stopped the Uruguayan civil war came to an abrupt end, and the two opposing parties within the country began to prepare for renewed conflict. The Uruguayan liberals were supported by Brazil, while the Uruguayan conservatives were backed by Paraguay. In 1863, war broke out once again in Uruguay, between the liberals of Venancio Flores and the conservatives of Bernardo Berro (who held power at that moment). Initially, the Brazilians attempted to mediate between the two sides, but in the end the conservatives rejected all forms of compromise. As a result, in 1864, the Brazilian Army crossed the border with Uruguay and intervened in open support of Flores—the *casus belli* that led to the beginning of the Paraguayan War.

### The unification of Argentina

Argentina was one of the first South American countries to become independent from Spain, with the May Revolution of 1810. The new nation played a critical role in the ensuing wars of independence of other South American nations, contributing in a decisive way to the liberation of Chile and Peru. Argentina, however, faced serious internal problems from the outset: Buenos Aires, the capital of the new republic, dominated the other provinces and thus sought to exert complete control over the territories located in the country's interior. Buenos Aires possessed the only port in Argentina that could be used effectively for commerce with the rest of the world, and this gave the inhabitants of the city a great advantage over the other Argentines from the interior regions.

This duality between Buenos Aires and the other provinces resulted in the formation of two political parties, which soon became the main protagonists of Argentine political life. The first of these was the Unitarian Party, which defended the interests of Buenos Aires: the *Unitarios* wanted to transform Argentina into a centralized state with power centered on the capital, and had liberal ideas. The second was the Federalist Party, which defended the interests of all the other Argentine provinces: the *Federales* wanted to transform Argentina into a federal state with considerable autonomy for the local territories, and had conservative ideas. The *Unitarios* were traditional allies of the Uruguayan liberals, while the *Federales* were supported by the Uruguayan conservatives.

One of the main political issues that caused friction between the *Unitarios* and *Federales* comprised the benefits deriving from the customs duties imposed by the port of Buenos Aires: the Unitarian Party wished to retain all the revenue in the Argentine capital, while the Federalists demanded the distribution of these external commercial taxes among all the Argentine provinces. Buenos Aires had a monopoly over trade with foreign countries, but the products that were exchanged and sold came from the interior provinces. As a result, Argentine political life was full of tensions from the outset. The first military clash between *Unitarios* and *Federales* took place as early as 1820. In 1828, once the Cisplatine War with Brazil had come to an end, a new civil war broke out. The victor to emerge from this conflict was the *Unitarios* leader Juan Lavalle; the *Unitarios*, however, were not able to hold on to power for long.

In 1829, Juan Manuel de Rosas, by now supreme commander of the *Federales*, took control of Buenos Aires and defeated Lavalle. During the following two decades, despite having to face down several other leaders of the Unitarian Party and deal with an Anglo-French naval blockade of the River Plate, de Rosas was able to maintain his grip on power and see off any internal or external threats. In 1851, however, he had to face opposition from his own political party: de Urquiza, one of the Federalist leaders, rose up in revolt against him and sought help from Brazil and Uruguay (the latter having just come under control of the liberals). As a result, in 1852 the coalition formed against de Rosas was able to achieve a brilliant victory at the Battle of Caseros on February 3, and de Urquiza thus became the new ruler of Argentina.

The *Unitarios*, however, were not going to accept a new era of Federalist rule after long decades of de Rosas' dictatorship. On September 11, 1852, Buenos Aires province seceded from the rest of Argentina and declared independence as the autonomous State of Buenos Aires. War between the Argentine Confederation and the State of Buenos Aires was merely a question of time. On October 3, 1859, de Urquiza and his *Federales* were able to defeat the *Unitarios* at the Battle of Cepeda, but this victory did not

An Argentine soldier of the 1º Legión de Voluntários (1st Legion of Volunteers). This unit was akin to a Foreign Legion, comprising volunteers and mercenaries of various nationalities, but mostly Italians. (Drawing by Benedetto Esposito; author's collection)

prove decisive. The two sides found a temporary compromise, which gave the *Unitarios* enough time to reorganize themselves for a new campaign. In 1861, the leader of Buenos Aires, Bartolomé Mitre, rejected the peace agreements and initiated new hostilities. This time, the military operations were favorable to the State of Buenos Aires: at the Battle of Pavón, on September 17, 1861, Mitre decisively defeated de Urquiza. As a result, in 1862, Argentina was again unified as a single nation and Mitre was elected as President of the Republic.

From 1863, the new Argentine government began to support the Uruguayan liberals in their civil war on the Eastern Bank; Mitre was a personal friend of Flores and the Argentines feared the Paraguayans acquiring a prominent role in the politics of Uruguay. Argentina was not prepared for a new war against an external enemy, and thus the support given to Flores was never officially sanctioned. Eventually, strong diplomatic pressure from Paraguay would lead to Argentine intervention in the new conflict.

### The Uruguayan civil wars

As noted above, Uruguay became an independent republic in 1828. Its capital was Montevideo, one of the most important ports on the Atlantic coast of South America, together with Buenos Aires. In broad terms, the existence of Uruguay was the result of a difficult compromise between Brazil and Argentina; this fact had significant consequences for the internal politics of the young republic, which was soon ravaged by the clash between conservatives (known as *Blancos*, or Whites) and liberals (the *Colorados*, or Reds). Hostilities between these two political parties broke out on a large scale in 1836: the *Blancos*, led by Manuel Oribe, defended the agricultural interests of the rural regions; the *Colorados*, led by José Fructuoso Rivera, represented the interests of Montevideo's commercial community. The political situation in Uruguay was thus very similar to the one in contemporary Argentina, and this frequently led to fusion between the civil wars of the two countries. Oribe was the most important external ally of de Rosas, while the Montevidean liberals could count on the support of the Argentine *Unitarios*.

In the first phase of the war, Rivera, in part thanks to military aid provided by France and by the secessionist Republic of Río Grande do Sul, secured a series of victories, and was thus able to expel Oribe from Uruguay. The leader of the *Blancos*, however, fled to Buenos Aires and sought the help of his ally de Rosas. In 1842, Oribe returned to Uruguay at the head of a large army provided to him by the Argentine dictator; thanks to his new military superiority, the *Blancos* leader defeated Rivera at the critical Battle of Arroyo Grande on December 6. After this clash, the remaining *Colorados* forces retreated back to Montevideo, where they were besieged by Oribe's army. The ensuing siege, commonly known as the Great Siege of Montevideo, lasted from 1843 to 1851. Against all odds, the defenders were able to resist for this lengthy period, mostly thanks to the decisive naval support provided by Britain and France, but also to the important role played by the Italian revolutionary leader Giuseppe Garibaldi. The siege came to an end when de Urquiza rose up against de Rosas in Argentina; like his ally, Oribe was defeated and Uruguay

An Argentine soldier of the Legión Militar, a military unit that had been formed in 1856 as the Legión Agrícola Militar. This was a volunteer corps of Italian immigrants who served as settlers and soldiers along the frontier with indigenous peoples (the "Indian Frontier") at Bahía Blanca. (Drawing by Benedetto Esposito; author's collection)

came under control of the *Colorados*. The latter then joined the military coalition formed during the Platine War, in order to remove once and for all the threat represented by de Rosas.

A period of stability—albeit brief—followed for Uruguay, lasting until 1855, when new tensions arose between the conservatives and the liberals. Open conflict broke out in 1863, when the *Colorados* rose up under the leadership of Venancio Flores; at that time, the *Blancos* controlled the Uruguayan government. Flores presented his revolution as a "crusade" against oppression, which came to be known as the *Cruzada Libertadora*. Initially, Flores encountered many difficulties in fighting the *Blancos* due to the latter's military superiority. Brazil remained neutral during this period and tried to stop the conflict by proposing a new compromise. The Uruguayan conservatives, however, refused any possible reconciliation and continued to fight against Flores with all their resources.

In 1864, when it became apparent that the *Blancos* were supported by Paraguay, Brazil decided to intervene in the Uruguayan conflict and openly sided with the *Colorados*. This was the beginning of the Uruguayan War, the main *casus belli* of the Paraguayan War. As we will see, the Brazilian intervention in Uruguay was decisive for Flores' final victory. In many respects, the Uruguayan War and the Paraguayan War can be considered as part of the same larger conflict. Most of the Paraguayan early victories in 1864 and 1865 were due to the fact that the majority of the Brazilian Army was still fighting in Uruguay. For this reason, the Brazilian military intervention in the Uruguayan War will be discussed in this book as part of the Paraguayan War.

The final moments of the Brazilian siege of Paysandú, a decisive event in the Uruguayan War of 1863–64.

# CHRONOLOGY

**1862**

September 10: Francisco Solano López succeeds his father, being unanimously proclaimed President of Paraguay for a term of ten years by the Paraguayan Congress.

October 12: Bartolomé Mitre is elected President of the Argentine Republic; Argentine national unity is finally restored after decades of civil war.

**1863**

April 19: Venancio Flores of the liberal *Colorados* party (favored by both Brazil and Argentina) launches a revolution in Uruguay against President Bernardo Berro of the conservative *Blancos* party (supported by Paraguay).

**1864**

October 12: The Brazilian Army intervenes in the Uruguayan Civil War, in order to support Flores in his struggle against the *Blancos*.

November 12: The Paraguayan warship *Tacuarí* captures the Brazilian ship *Marquês de Olinda*, which has sailed up the Paraguay River to the Brazilian province of Mato Grosso.

November 13: The Paraguayan Army starts preparations for the invasion of Mato Grosso province.

December 13: Paraguay declares war on Brazil; beginning of the Paraguayan War.

December 27: Paraguayan incursions into Mato Grosso begin.

**1865**

January 2: The strategic port of Paysandú in Uruguay is captured after a 35-day siege by Flores and his Brazilian allies.

January 14: The Argentine president Mitre rejects López's request for Paraguayan troops to be allowed passage through Argentina's Corrientes province, in order to invade Uruguay.

February 22: Venancio Flores and the *Colorados* enter the Uruguayan capital of Montevideo. The Uruguayan Civil War is over.

March 18: Paraguay declares war on Argentina.

April 14: Paraguayan forces invade Corrientes province.

May 1: The Triple Alliance Treaty is signed between Brazil, Argentina, and Uruguay. President Mitre is appointed commander-in-chief of the Alliance military forces.

May 25: Argentine forces retake the city of Corrientes, expelling the Paraguayans.

May 26: A strong Paraguayan relief force reaches Corrientes, obliging the Argentines to abandon the city and reoccupy their former positions.

June 11: The decisive naval battle of the Riachuelo is fought on the Paraná River opposite Corrientes city, between the Paraguayan and Brazilian fleets. The clash, which remains the largest naval battle in the history of South America, results in an emphatic Brazilian victory and the total annihilation of Paraguay's naval forces.

June 12: The Paraguayans begin the invasion of the Brazilian province of Río Grande do Sul, occupying the city of São Borja.

August 5: The Paraguayan Army occupies the key town of Uruguayana, located on the Uruguay River in Río Grande do Sul province.

August 17: The Battle of Yatay, in Río Grande do Sul. Some 3,200 Paraguayans are emphatically defeated by a 10,000-strong Alliance Army.

September 18: The Paraguayan garrison in Uruguayana, numbering 8,000 men, surrenders to the besieging Alliance army. The Paraguayans are expelled from Río Grande do Sul province.

October 3: The Argentines defeat the enemy forces stationed in the Paraguayan province of Misiones, and occupy the territory bordering Río Grande do Sul.

**1865/66** Autumn/winter: López concentrates all his previously dispersed forces along the northern bank of the Paraná River. The Alliance Army builds its encampment opposite the Paraguayans on the southern bank of the river. Military operations slow down for several months.

**1866** April 16–19: Fighting at Itapirú results in a Paraguayan defeat, which enables the Alliance to begin crossing the Paraná, near its confluence with the Paraguay River. The Paraguayans make no serious attempts to oppose the crossing operations, which are successful.

May 2: The Battle of Estero Bellaco, involving 6,000 Paraguayan and 8,000 Alliance soldiers. An Alliance victory, but both sides suffer high casualties. The Alliance then stops at Tuyutí, where it builds an immense camp that is partly protected by entrenchments and field fortifications.

May 24: The First Battle of Tuyutí, fought between 24,000 Paraguayans and 35,000 Alliance troops—the

greatest field battle in the history of South America. The Paraguayan attack against the Alliance camp is repulsed with crippling losses (around 13,000 men).

July 10–11: The Battle of Yataytí Corá, an Alliance victory.

July 16–18: The Battle of Boquerón del Sauce. The Alliance suffers high casualties.

September 1–3: The Alliance attacks and captures the Paraguayan fort of Curuzú.

September 12: Peace talks of Yataytí Corá between López and Mitre; the Argentine president rejects the idea of a separate peace with Paraguay.

September 22: The Battle of Curupaytí, the most important Paraguayan victory in the war. The Alliance assault on the Paraguayan defensive positions is repulsed with terrible losses (4,000 soldiers killed).

**October 1866–** **July 1867** A stalemate for ten months. The Alliance returns to its encampment at Tuyutí, while López prepares new defenses. Diseases, including cholera and typhoid, spread throughout the camps, causing thousands of deaths.

**1867** August–October: The Alliance Army maneuvers to isolate the formidable fortress of Humaitá, in order to cut its lines of communication and supply from Asunción. Humaitá, known as the Paraguayan Sebastopol, has an extensive complex of brick-built bastions and casemates mounting 62 artillery pieces of different caliber, distributed among eight batteries. These are built on a superb defensive site commanding a sharp S-bend in the Paraguay River (10m above the level of the river), most of them dominating narrows which are protected by a massive chain-boom and two lines of explosive mines.

November 2: The indecisive Second Battle of Tuyutí; a Paraguayan attack against the Alliance camp is repulsed.

**1868**

January 18: The Brazilian Duke of Caxias becomes the new commander-in-chief of the Alliance Army.

February 19: The Brazilian fleet bombards Humaitá and forces a passage upriver. The long Alliance siege of Humaitá begins.

March 23: The Paraguayan defensive position at Curupaytí falls.

July 26: Cut off from all sides and running out of food and ammunition, the Humaitá garrison finally abandons its positions.

September: The Paraguayans fall back to a new fortified defensive line, stretching along the Pikysyry Stream from the strong river batteries at Angostura.

December: Caxias launches the *Dezembrada*, the Alliance assault against the Pikysyry defensive line. Rather than attempting frontal attacks, Caxias ships a large part of his forces across to the west bank of the Paraguay River and has them build a corduroy (log) road for some miles through the marshes to take them north. He then ships them back to the east bank, well behind the enemy positions and ready to attack the Paraguayan forces. This is the famous Pikysyry Maneuver.

December 6: Alliance victory at Ytororó; the Paraguayans lose 1,000 men.

December 12: Alliance victory at Avay; the Paraguayans lose 5,000 men.

December 24: López rejects surrender terms.

December 25: Alliance victory at Ypacaraí; López flees to Cerro León.

December 21–27: Alliance victory at Lomas Valentinas/Itá Ibaté; the Paraguayans are defeated with heavy losses.

December 30: The Paraguayan defensive position of Angostura surrenders.

**1869**

January 1: The Alliance enters the Paraguayan capital of Asunción.

January–July: López withdraws into the eastern highlands of Paraguay to continue his hopeless fight. His few remaining soldiers are hungry, ragged, and short of every supply.

August 12: Alliance victory at Peribebuy.

August 16: Alliance victory at Acosta Ñu/Campo Grande, the last significant battle of the war. Some 2,000 Paraguayan soldiers are killed and 1,500 captured.

December 28: After various skirmishes, López, by now a fugitive with just a few hundred followers, begins his final retreat to the densely forested mountains of the Paraguayan northeast.

**1870**

March 1: The Brazilians catch up with and defeat López's few remaining followers at Cerro Corá. The death of López during this skirmish brings the Paraguayan War to an end.

# OPPOSING COMMANDERS

## PARAGUAYAN

**Francisco Solano López** was born in 1827. At the tender age of 18, he was commissioned as a brigadier-general in the Paraguayan Army. The following year, the future "Napoleon of La Plata" was appointed commander-in-chief of the Paraguayan military contingent sent to assist Corrientes province in its rebellion against the Argentine dictator de Rosas. This was the first experience of field command for López, but it ended in complete disaster (the Paraguayans showing their indiscipline, and failing to take part in any proper military action). Francisco Solano López then continued his military studies in Asunción and Río de Janeiro (at that time Paraguay was on friendly terms with Brazil), and in particular showed great interest in the technical fields of artillery and fortifications.

The political and military leaders of Uruguay, Argentina, and Paraguay: from left to right, Venancio Flores, Bartolomé Mitre, and Francisco Solano López.

The Paraguayan dictator Francisco Solano López in full dress uniform. The latter shows the strong influence of the military fashions of France's Napoleon III, which at that time were dominant in South America.

Portrait of the veteran general José Vicente Barrios, one of the most important commanders in the Paraguayan Army. Barrios led one of the attacking columns at the Battle of Tuyutí.

In 1853, López was sent to Europe by his father, as minister plenipotentiary: his mission was to conduct a series of diplomatic encounters in order to secure powerful allies for Paraguay. He traveled across Europe, visiting several countries (Great Britain, France, and the Kingdom of Sardinia), and stayed abroad for a year and a half, which he spent mostly in Paris. In the French capital, he attended military classes as a guest student in the École spéciale militaire de Saint-Cyr (at that time, the best military school in the world). During his stay in Paris, López earned the personal admiration of the French emperor Napoleon III; the latter granted him the honor of leading a large military parade, and awarded him the Légion d'honneur.

The future Paraguayan leader then went to the Crimea, as a military observer attached to the French contingent. This was a very important experience for Francisco Solano López, who was able to witness the latest military field innovations. The Paraguayan diplomatic mission in Europe also had other objectives: purchasing modern weapons for the army and steamers for the navy, importing new technologies, and finding foreign technical experts willing to serve in Paraguay. When Francisco Solano López later returned to Paraguay, he used what he had seen to improve the infrastructure of his country (with one eye on potential military uses for this): a new and efficient railroad was begun, as was the first electric telegraph system in South America. López's time in France also had enduring effects on his personality: he developed a fascination with the Imperial French military world, especially for the figures of Napoleon I and Napoleon III. He also met Eliza Lynch, an Irish-born courtesan, who later became his concubine and traveled to Paraguay.

In 1855, Francisco Solano López returned to his native country and was appointed minister of war by his father (becoming the supreme commander of the Paraguayan Army). In 1857, he was elevated to the office of vice president, thus becoming one of the most powerful men in South America. During the final years of his father's rule, Francisco Solano López tried to improve the quality of the Paraguayan military in every possible way (notably by recruiting foreign advisors). In 1862, he was elected President of Paraguay by the National Congress for a term of ten years; he was well loved by the people, and had the unwavering support of the army. As events would soon show, he did not lack military competence but his aspirations for Paraguay were impossible to achieve for such a small nation.

López could count on several reliable military commanders, despite the fact that the Paraguayan Army had never been involved in a

large conflict before 1864. Among these were **Vicente Barrios** (1825–68) and **Bernardino Caballero** (1839–1912). The former began his military career in 1843, and became a captain just four years later. In 1853, he was appointed lieutenant-colonel, and later accompanied Francisco Solano López on his travels across Europe. Barrios learned French and increased his military knowledge. He married López's sister Innocentia, and thus became one of Paraguay's most important political and military leaders.

The Duke of Caxias ordering the Brazilian charge at the Battle of Lomas Valentinas, fought on December 27, 1868.

At the beginning of the war, in 1864, Caballero was a young ensign and the personal aide-de-camp of Francisco Solano López. Thanks to his intelligence, and despite his very little combat experience, he rose to become one of the Paraguayan Army's most important leaders within the space of a few months. Caballero proved to be an excellent cavalry commander and was soon promoted after fighting with great courage at Estero Bellaco. In contrast to Barrios, who was killed in 1868 after being suspected of treason by López, Caballero had a long military career, and eventually became President of Paraguay several years after the end of the war, being considered a true national hero.

# TRIPLE ALLIANCE

## *Brazilian*

For a large part of the Paraguayan War, the most important military commander in the Brazilian Army was the **Duke of Caxias (Luís Alves de Lima e Silva)**. Born in 1803, he was descended from a line of Portuguese officers; his forebears had settled in Brazil in the 1760s. The future commander-in-chief of the Brazilian Army began his military career as early as 1808, when he was enlisted as a cadet in the 1st Infantry Regiment of Río de Janeiro (both his father and grandfather had previously served in this unit). In 1818, the future duke entered the prestigious Royal Military Academy of Río de Janeiro, which formed the elite of the Brazilian officer corps. Two years later, he was already a 1st lieutenant. During the Brazilian War of Independence, Luís took part in the hostilities on the side of Pedro I (as did the rest of his family) and fought as a junior officer against the Portuguese garrisons that were stationed in the province of Bahia. In the ensuing years, he took part in the Cisplatine War against Argentina, and remained loyal to the new monarchy.

The decade following Pedro I's abdication was marked by serious internal troubles in Brazil, with the country governed by a regent. Popular revolts and military mutinies were frequent, and the situation was generally unstable. During these turbulent years, Luís Alves de Lima e Silva reached the top of the Brazilian military hierarchy, thanks both to his competence and great loyalty toward Pedro II. In the late 1830s, he was appointed as instructor in swordmanship and horsemanship to the young emperor,

The Count of Eu (with hand on hip) and his staff in 1870. On March 22, 1869, the young count was made commander-in-chief of the Alliance armies, after the Duke of Caxias renounced that position. This delegation of authority was based on the count's prestige as an officer of high rank, as well as on his reputation and skill in military action.

which formed a strong personal bond between the two young men that would continue for the rest of their lives.

In 1839, the future Duke of Caxias was promoted colonel, and quelled the rural Balaiada rebellion in Maranhão province. In 1841, he obtained the title of Baron of Caxias and became a brigadier-general (he would become a duke in 1869). In 1842, Luís Alves de Lima e Silva had a prominent role in defeating the new liberal uprisings, and thus helped Pedro II to retain his throne. Between 1842 and 1845, the Baron of Caxias played a prominent role during the final phase of Río Grande do Sul's secessionist rebellion. Using counterinsurgency tactics, Caxias' successes ended the long conflict once and for all. By this time, he had become a rich aristocrat, owning large plantations and hundreds of slaves. In 1851, Caxias took part in the Platine War, as the second-in-command of the Brazilian Army. In 1865, when the Paraguayans attacked Brazil's southern provinces, Caxias went to the front together with Pedro II, and later assumed supreme command of Brazil's military forces.

In the closing months of the Paraguayan War, the Alliance Army was commanded by the **Count of Eu (Prince Gaston of Orléans, 1842–1922)**. He was a French aristocrat and military officer who had married Isabel, daughter of Pedro II and heiress to the Brazilian throne. Being part of the French royal family, the young Gaston had been trained as a military officer (in the Spanish Army) from a young age, and became an artillery expert. He took part in the most important clashes of the Hispano-Moroccan War of 1859–60, before moving to Brazil in 1864 to marry

Princess Isabel. Until March 1869, the Count of Eu was not permitted to act as front-line commander, but this changed when he was given command of the Alliance Army with precise orders to capture or kill Francisco Solano López.

### Argentine

**Bartolomé Mitre** was commander-in-chief of the Argentine military forces and of the Alliance Army during the opening years of the Paraguayan War. Born in 1821, he held strongly liberal views from the outset of his early career both as a journalist and as a soldier. In those years, Argentina was dominated by the conservatives and by their leader de Rosas; as a result, Mitre was obliged to live as an exile in the Uruguayan capital Montevideo. There, he soon became one of the leading supporters of the *Colorados* liberal leader Rivera. In 1846, Rivera made Mitre a lieutenant-colonel in the Uruguayan Army, and the Argentine patriot participated in the Uruguayan Civil War between Oribe and Rivera.

After the final defeat of de Rosas at the Battle of Caseros on February 3, 1852, Mitre returned to Argentina. At that time the new master of the country was de Urquiza, the federalist leader supported by Brazil. Mitre soon became one of the leading *Unitarios* who rejected the new government, and when the province of Buenos Aires seceded from the Argentine Confederation in 1852, Mitre covered several important positions in the new independent administration. He also commanded the military forces of the latter during the Battle of Cepeda in 1859, where he was defeated by the much more experienced de Urquiza; however, the peace terms that followed the battle were positive for the State of Buenos Aires. In May 1860, Mitre became Governor of Buenos Aires, assuming complete control over the Argentine *Unitarios*. In 1861, the military forces of Buenos Aires, under Mitre's personal command, decisively defeated de Urquiza and his army; as a result, Argentina was again unified as a single nation. In 1862, the *Unitarios* leader was elected as President of the Argentine Confederation.

The path ahead for the Argentine nation presented numerous problems: after more than three decades of civil war, the country's economy and social infrastructure had almost collapsed. In addition, de Urquiza's conservatives were still ready to rise in open rebellion should the central government falter or fail. Mitre attempted to fix all these issues, and to avoid the outbreak of a new civil war. In 1864, when the Uruguayan crisis led to the Brazilian military intervention, he attempted to remain neutral. Both Paraguay and

Justo José de Urquiza, President of the Argentine Confederation between 1852 and 1861. During the period of the Paraguayan War, Urquiza went back to his home province of Entre Ríos and served as the local governor. Mitre feared an alliance between the Paraguayans and Urquiza; however, fortunately for him, this never materialized.

Brazil wanted Argentina as an ally, but Mitre was well aware that his country was ill prepared for war. Strong Paraguayan pressure and the invasion of Corrientes province, however, obliged the Argentine leader to side with the Brazilians and with his old friend Flores, thus forming the Triple Alliance.

During the Paraguayan War, Mitre counted on the decisive support of a highly experienced general, **Wenceslao Paunero** (1805–71). He had joined the Argentine Army in 1825, and had fought through the 1825–28 Cisplatine War against Brazil. During the long years of the Argentine civil wars, Paunero consistently opposed de Rosas, and was thus obliged to live in exile in Bolivia for a lengthy period. In 1851, he returned to Argentina and contributed to the fall of de Rosas by taking part in the decisive Battle of Caseros. A personal friend of Mitre, when Buenos Aires became an independent state he fought against de Urquiza. After Mitre's final victory, Paunero became the most important commander of the Argentine Army, and served for the duration of the Paraguayan War.

### Uruguayan

Born in 1808, **Venancio Flores** became one of the *Colorados* political and military leaders while relatively young. He fought during the long Uruguayan Civil War on the side of Rivera, opposing Oribe during the Siege of Montevideo. His charisma and military knowledge led him to become a leading figure in the Uruguayan Liberal Party. After the victory at Caseros and the fall of de Rosas, the *Colorados* assumed control of Uruguay and reached a compromise with the *Blancos*. In 1853, the country was ruled by a triumvirate of the three most important Liberal leaders: Rivera, Flores, and Juan Antonio Lavalleja.

Flores briefly served as president of the Uruguayan Republic until being removed by a new *Blancos* uprising. Flores went to Argentina and mashalled his supporters in preparation for a new civil war against the conservatives. In 1863, thanks to the support received from his personal friend Bartolomé Mitre, Flores returned to Uruguay and launched his *Cruzada Libertadora*. Initially, the *Colorados* struggled to defeat the *Blancos* and thus Flores had to ask for direct support from his foreign allies. In 1864, when Brazil invaded Uruguay from the north, Flores' military forces joined the Brazilian Army and gradually besieged all the strongholds still in the hands of his internal enemies. When Uruguay was finally liberated from the *Blancos*, Flores joined the Triple Alliance formed against Paraguay, and served as a leading field commander, often in the vanguard.

In 1864, the core of the Uruguayan Army was formed by the Florida Battalion, a unit of battle-hardened veterans. Its commander was the courageous **León de Pallejas** (1816–66), an experienced Spanish military officer who had fought with distinction during the bloody First Carlist War of 1833–40. After the Carlist defeat, de Pallejas emigrated to Uruguay and fought in the long Siege of Montevideo. In 1852, he took part in the Battle of Caseros against de Rosas, commanding one of the Uruguayan infantry battalions. He became a personal friend of Venancio Flores, and was his most important military commander. After playing a key role in the *Cruzada Libertadora*, he was dispatched to the Paraguayan War front at the head of the elite Florida Battalion.

# OPPOSING FORCES

## PARAGUAYAN

In 1863, the Paraguayan Army comprised 7,000 men organized into seven infantry battalions, five cavalry regiments, three artillery regiments (two of light/mounted artillery, and one of siege artillery), and a battalion of marines. The soldiers of the 6th and 7th Infantry battalions also acted as *zapadores* (sappers), since the army had no separate units of engineers.

Each infantry battalion theoretically numbered 1,000 men at full strength, organized into five line companies, a light company, and a reserve company. Each cavalry regiment, at least nominally, had four squadrons of two companies each. The regiments of light artillery were structured around four batteries with six guns each, while the siege artillery regiment had four companies with six heavy guns each. The Paraguayan Army also had a number of independent cavalry squadrons serving on the frontiers or in other garrisons. López could also rely on the Police Battalion based in the capital, which was 576 strong, and on the other police companies distributed throughout national territory.

As a result of Brazil's military intervention in the Uruguayan Civil War of 1864, Solano López decided to build a military encampment along the border with Brazil. In March that year, after conducting an inspection near Paraguarí, he ordered the construction of the Cerro León encampment. All Paraguayan citizens of military age (16–40) were called up to serve in the army, and gathered at the new camp. By December 1864, the Paraguayan Army had completed its expansion and comprised 30 infantry battalions, 23 cavalry regiments, and four regiments of artillery (each with 24 field pieces). In a few months, López had transformed the Paraguayan Army into the largest and best-trained military force in South America. All the infantry battalions now had six companies of 100 men each, of which the first four were grenadiers (comprising the tallest and best

A Paraguayan soldier with his corporal (left) and an old veteran saluting his superior officer (right), from a contemporary engraving dating back to 1867. Paraguayan corporals meted out punishments and seemingly always kept their sticks at the ready. In general, discipline was very strict: the punishment regulations followed old Spanish ordinances and relied heavily on canings or beatings.

A Brazilian engraving from 1868, showing the contemporary uniforms of the Paraguayan Army. The figure to the right has a traditional turu on his back, a musical instrument made out of a bull's horn by the Guaraní Indians of Paraguay.

men) and the fifth and sixth *cazadores* (elite light infantry). By March 1865, a further eight infantry battalions and six cavalry regiments had been organized. As a result, by the time war broke out with Argentina, the Paraguayan Army had a force of 38,137 men divided into 38 infantry battalions, 29 cavalry regiments, three regiments of campaign artillery, and a regiment of siege artillery. Two elite cavalry regiments, known as the Acá Carayá and Acá Verá, provided the presidential guard for Solano López, acting as his mounted escort.

Campaign artillery was served by the cavalry and had only small guns, and was commonly known as horse or light artillery. Siege artillery (known as heavy or fortress artillery) was served by the infantry. Each battery of horse artillery in theory had four cannons and two howitzers, but during the war, each battery might only possess two to four guns in total.

In contrast with the Allies, by the time of the War of the Triple Alliance, Paraguay no longer possessed a National Guard. As a result, as hostilities progressed, Solano López could only rely on a general militia, which potentially comprised all the able-bodied men in the country, the age limits being soon forgotten in the face of the severe lack of manpower. During the final phase of the conflict, even young boys and elderly veterans were called to serve in the army's ranks.

### Weaponry

The Paraguayan Army's weapons were mostly antique, obsolete, and in poor repair due to many years of use. The standard infantry weapons were the old Dupont and Brown Bess flintlock muskets, of which 20,000 had been bought (mainly from Brazil) between 1845 and 1850 and then distributed to the soldiers gathered at Cerro León in 1864. Only three infantry battalions had Witton or Enfield percussion rifles, which had been purchased in 1863. Cavalrymen were usually armed with 9ft-long lances, and sabers. Many of the latter were of the old, stirrup-hilted British Pattern 1796 for light cavalry, or local copies of it. Flintlock carbines were rare and issued only to some regiments. The Acá Carayá and Acá Verá were armed with Turner and Witton rifled carbines. The *bolas*, used to entangle the legs of enemy horses, were very common in Paraguayan mounted units.

The Paraguayan field artillery had just one battery of rifled 12-lb guns, purchased in 1863; all the others were iron or bronze smoothbores of different calibers (*carronadas*), ranging from 2 to 32 lb. The fortress artillery had 24 cannons of 8in., two of 56 lb, and a further 100 pieces of various calibers and weights (most of these ranging from 24 lb to 32 lb, or from 8 lb to 12 lb). The largest pieces were mounted at the Fortress of Humaitá. Many of the Paraguayan guns dated back to the colonial period, or were cast locally. Several field guns were taken from the Brazilian forts in Mato Grosso during the invasion of 1864. The Paraguayan government had ordered new guns from France and Prussia, but because of the Brazilian

naval blockade these did not reach Paraguay. In addition, rocket-launchers are also mentioned at several actions—presumably locally manufactured Congreve and/or Hales models.

Brazilian soldiers of the 26th Corpo de Voluntários da Pátria from Ceará Province, conducting skirmishing in Paraguayan territory.

# TRIPLE ALLIANCE

## Brazilian Army

In 1864, the Brazilian Army consisted of 14 infantry battalions, five cavalry regiments, four battalions of foot artillery, a (battalion-sized) corps of horse artillery, an engineer battalion, and a corps of artificers. In total, there were 1,733 officers and 15,091 other ranks.

Of the 14 infantry battalions, the first through seventh were line infantry (*fuzileiros*) and the eighth through fourteenth were *caçadores*. Each line infantry battalion totaled 882 men and had eight companies; the light infantry ones totaled 552 men divided into six companies. The regiments of cavalry, totaling 618 men each, had four squadrons of three companies each. One squadron was armed with carbines, and the other three lances. Each of the foot artillery battalions had 690 men in eight companies, while the Horse Artillery Corps had four companies with 557 men. The Engineer Battalion was structured around four companies.

The regular forces were supported by the "Fixed" corps (garrison units) and by the National Guard. In 1865, Decree No. 3,383 mobilized 14,796 *Guardias Nacionales* for war service; some were sent to join the regular army in the field, others to perform policing duties behind the lines or to relieve regular troops in provincial garrisons.

A Brazilian sapper from the National Guard of the Court, wearing his elegant parade dress including bearskin, gloves, jaguar skin, and apron (bearing the Brazilian imperial coat-of-arms). (Benedetto Esposito; author's collection)

In 1866, the Brazilian Army was expanded and reorganized. All the Fixed corps were disbanded and incorporated into the regular forces, with their soldiers being used as cadres for new regular units. A further eight infantry battalions were formed, all of *caçadores*, for a total of 22. The 4th and 5th Cavalry regiments were broken up and used as cadres to form five new corps of *Caçadores a Cavallo* (Mounted Rifles), each having 638 men in four squadrons. A 5th Battalion of Foot Artillery was raised, and the Horse Artillery Corps had to provide a cadre for the formation of a second Provisional Corps. The Battalion of Engineers remained basically unchanged, but at a higher establishment. Also, in 1865, a Train Squadron had been added to the technical units. In addition to these forces, the Brazilians also had a strong corps of naval infantry, created in 1808; from 1852, this was known as the *Batalhão Naval* (Naval Battalion). This numbered 1,845 soldiers, 1,428 of whom took part to the war in Paraguay (843 naval infantrymen and 585 naval artillerymen).

Although the empire had a large National Guard, Brazilian law stated that its individual provincial units could only be used beyond the national borders when their respective home provinces were attacked by external forces. The Paraguayan attacks against Mato Grosso and Río Grande do Sul therefore meant that only those two provinces could send National Guard units to assist the regular army in the field. As a result of this situation, the Brazilian government opted for the creation of a whole new class of volunteer troops, organized separately from the National Guard, and intended to last for the duration of the war with Paraguay. With Decree No. 3,371 of January 7, 1865, the emperor ordered the formation of the new *Corpo de Voluntários da Pátria*. There was an enthusiastic response to the creation of this new force: thousands of men from all over the country answered the call within a short period of time and signed up. In total, during the Paraguayan War, Brazil mobilized a total of 55,985 volunteers.

### Weaponry

In 1857, the Brazilian Army had been re-equipped with new rifled percussion-lock weapons, all Belgian-made Minié. In 1858, a number of similar Enfield weapons were purchased from Great Britain. In general, the standard Brazilian weapons were Belgian, because the British ones were bought only in small numbers. The line infantry muskets were either Belgian Espingardas Minié or Pattern 1853 Enfields. In 1867, the Brazilian Army purchased 5,000 Roberts rifles, but these did not see service during the war due to ammunition problems. The *Caçadores* battalions were armed with the same weapons as the line infantry, but in the light infantry shorter version.

The Brazilian cavalry was armed with Minié or Enfield carbines, which were gradually replaced from 1867 by the excellent Spencer seven-shot carbine (2,000 of which had been purchased in 1866). Cavalrymen were also armed with model 1831 or 1851 sabers, which were Brazilian copies of the excellent French 1822 light cavalry saber. They also had lances, which were either the 1844 model (imported from Great Britain) or the 1864 model (imported from France).

Brazilian field artillery was technically up to date and consisted mainly of muzzle-loading rifled cannons of the French Model 1858 4-pdr La Hitte system, and British Whitworth 20-lb field guns. In addition, locally manufactured Congreve and Hales rockets were used.

### Argentine Army

On January 26, 1864, a presidential decree ordered the reorganization of the Argentine Army. The standing forces were reduced from 10,200 to 6,000 men, organized into six infantry battalions, eight cavalry regiments, and one artillery regiment. Each unit, regardless of branch of service, was to have an establishment of 400 soldiers. According to the new organization, each infantry battalion had five companies of 80 men: one of grenadiers, one of *cazadores*, and three of fusiliers. Each cavalry regiment had four squadrons with 100 men, divided into two companies. The Regiment of Artillery was organized into two squadrons of two batteries each, and had light horse-drawn guns.

A Brazilian cavalry officer (on the left) and an officer of the Voluntários da Pátria (on the right).

As soon as the Argentine Army implemented this severe reduction, Mitre was forced to decree a "Siege Status and War Situation" order in response to the Paraguayan declaration of war on April 16, 1865. As a result, the so-called Army of the Line was once again increased to 10,000 soldiers, organized into 11 infantry battalions, eight cavalry regiments, and a regiment of artillery. All the infantry battalions were increased in size to comprise six companies, with 80 men in each.

On April 20, 1865, a company of *zapadores* was added to Argentina's regular forces, composed of 100 volunteers from the National Guard of Buenos Aires; they were commanded by Colonel Juan Fernando Cetz, a Polish officer in the service of Argentina. On June 1, 1865, the unit was expanded and became the Battalion of Engineers. In addition to these regular forces, there were also two Legions of Volunteers, mainly formed of Italians; their organization followed that of the line battalions.

Shortly after the reorganization of the regular army, a new Mitre decree addressed the organization and composition of the Argentine National Guard. On April 17, 1865, the Argentine president declared the formation of the National Army on Campaign; this included the 10,000 soldiers of the regular army, plus 15,000 men from the National Guard. In total, this new force was to comprise 30 infantry battalions (11 of the line, and 19 of the National

A contemporary engraving showing the uniforms of the Argentine infantry. From left to right: an officer in parade uniform, a corporal in parade uniform, a soldier in summer uniform, and a soldier in service uniform.

A contemporary engraving showing the uniforms of the Argentine Army at the beginning of the War of the Triple Alliance. The figure on the left is presumably a staff officer, wearing a simple dark blue campaign uniform with kepi and epaulettes. The central figure is a cavalryman in parade dress, from the 3rd Cavalry Regiment. The figure on the right is an artilleryman in parade uniform.

Guard) with 500 soldiers in each battalion. Mitre also determined the quantity of the contingents that each province should provide, and that were sent to the capital for the war effort. Buenos Aires alone provided eight infantry battalions. This represented the most important contribution to the formation of the National Guard; in contrast with the majority of the other provinces, patriotic feelings were strong in Buenos Aires, and there was continued popular support for the war. The first four battalions were formed in the city of Buenos Aires from veterans of the last civil war; the other four were newly raised units from the province of Buenos Aires. The eight infantry battalions were grouped into two divisions of 2,000 men each: the veteran units made up the 1st Division, while the 2nd Division was composed of new units. Attached to each battalion of the 1st Division was a company of National Guard artillery.

In addition to these units, two other infantry battalions from Buenos Aires took part in the Paraguayan campaign: the first was the elite San Nicolás Battalion, and the second was the *3 de Oro* (Golden Three). The National Guard of Buenos Aires also raised two regiments of cavalry, formed with gauchos (skilled horsemen) from the south of the province. The first cavalry unit to be raised was the General San Martín Cavalry Regiment, followed just a month later by the General Lavalle Cavalry Regiment. Both units were divided into two squadrons, the first with 600 men and the second with only 400.

## Weaponry

At the outset of the Paraguayan War, the Argentine Army employed a bewildering variety of muzzle-loading muskets and a small number of modern breech-loaders. This presented a nightmarish situation for the supply branch and caused numerous problems during the conflict. The most common infantry weapon was the Brown Bess Model 1777 musket, locally known as a "Tower" because it bore the inspection seal of the Tower of London arsenal. More than 11,000 of these flintlock muskets had been captured from the British during the invasions of 1806–07. With the exception of the battalions from Buenos Aires (which had percussion muskets, like the majority of the regulars), all the National Guard infantrymen were armed with the Brown Bess. The percussion muskets, smoothbores, or rifles, were of different makes and calibers: 18mm French M1842T, French Minié M1851, 18mm Norwegian M1842, 17.8mm Thouvenin M1853 ("carabine à tige"), and 18mm Alem M1842 (manufactured in Germany, issued to the National Guard infantry of Buenos Aires).

In December 1865, six Pattern 1853 Enfields were dispatched to the front for evaluation. As a result of their positive performance, a limited number of them were purchased. After 1865, new breech-loading rifles were gradually purchased, but always in small quantities: these included British Snider-Enfield, Springfield M1859, French Tabatière M1867, Austrian Werndl M1867, Russian Berdan M1868, Belgian Gerard M1860, and surplus contract rifles of the American Civil War (Norwich, Trenton, and Whitney) that had been converted to the Roberts 1867 breech-loading system. In the final phase of the war, 8,000 Springfield M1861 rifles were purchased from the United States.

The cavalry used many different types of carbines, especially at the beginning of the war: Tower, 18mm French M1829T Bis (known as the "Vincennes"), 18mm French M1842T, 18mm Belgian M1842T, and 18mm French M1840 muskets cut down as carbines. In addition, a certain number of Pattern 1856 Enfield cavalry carbines and Pattern 1861 Enfield musketoons were also in use. Later in the war, Argentine cavalrymen received small numbers of breech-loading repeating carbines, most notably Spencers (models 1865 or 1867) and Sharps (the former given also to Mitre's escort). The regular cavalry had a certain number of Prussian model 1852 sabers, but the majority of Argentine cavalrymen (especially in the National Guard) were armed with old stirrup-hilted (Pattern 1796 for light cavalry) or Mameluke-hilted British sabers. The lances comprised the main weapon of the Argentine cavalry, and *bolas* were also very popular.

At the beginning of the war, there were 280 pieces of artillery in Argentina, distributed in various depots and garrisons throughout national territory. However, most of these had aging, pitted tubes and had a range of only 400–600m. In 1865, a limited number of these smoothbores were converted into rifled artillery by the firm of Antonio Massa, based in Buenos Aires. A Krupp 12-pdr mountain gun was purchased for evaluation purposes in July 1865, and, on the back of its positive field performance, a further 11 followed in 1867. Argentina was the first South American country to adopt the Krupp artillery system. During 1865 and 1866, the Argentines bought new Whitworth and Hotchkiss field guns: a battery of six rifled 6-pdrs, and a battery of six 20-pdr rifled steel guns. In April 1867, a Gatling machine gun was purchased from the United States.

An Argentine infantryman from the Buenos Aires National Guard, wearing the campaign dress used at the beginning of the war (with kepi and blouse). (Benedetto Esposito; author's collection)

## Uruguayan Army

In May 1865, after the signing of the Triple Alliance Treaty, Flores issued a series of decrees designed to increase the strength of Uruguay's armed forces. A June 1 decree detailed the composition of the Uruguayan contingent sent to the Paraguayan front: four infantry battalions (Florida, 24 de Abril, Voluntários de la Libertad, and Voluntários Auxiliares), three National Guard cavalry regiments, and one squadron of horse artillery (with two batteries). These Uruguayan forces were grouped in the so-called *División Oriental* (Oriental Division), which was under command of the same Venancio Flores. By the time the division left Montevideo, it had been joined by a squadron of regular cavalry—the Escolta—and was sent to provide Flores' mounted escort. In addition to the formation of the Oriental Division, Flores' decrees reconstituted the Uruguayan National Guard: according to them, each department of the country was ordered to raise a unit of 250 men. As a result, various regiments of National Guard cavalry and battalions of National Guard infantry were organized. The infantry battalions were left behind as garrisons in Uruguay, together with the 1st Battery of horse artillery from the regular army.

## Weaponry

Until the end of the Platine War of 1852, the Uruguayan Army was mostly equipped with flintlock muskets. Its government then began buying small numbers of new and more modern weapons. These included Saint-Etienne percussion rifles M1854 and M1857, plus a certain number of Pattern 1853 Enfield rifles and carbines. When the Paraguayan War broke out, Uruguayan infantrymen were equipped with a mixture of firearms: percussion, flintlock, rifled, and non-rifled weapons. For example, we know that two companies of the 24 de Abril Battalion had flintlocks, while the rest of the unit was armed with percussion muskets. Shortly before its departure from Montevideo, the Florida Battalion received new Minié rifles: these were known in Uruguay as Model n.1 rifles. On October 24, 1865, both the Florida and 24 de Abril battalions were re-equipped with new Minié rifles, the so-called Model n.2. As the war progressed, the whole Uruguayan Army was rearmed with Minié Model n.2 rifles. In the last phase of the conflict, a few Remington M1863/64 rolling blocks saw service with the Uruguayan Army.

Initially, the artillery of the Oriental Division had just eight guns: two rifled 4-pdrs, two 6-pdrs, and four 9-pdrs. After the fall of Uruguayana, it was augmented with two 6-pdrs captured from the Paraguayans. On July 2, 1866, the Uruguayan artillery was further augmented with four 12-pdrs transferred by the Brazilians. Following the surrender of the Paraguayan defensive line at Angostura, on December 30, 1868, the Uruguayans received some of the Paraguayan captured guns. These were mostly iron smoothbores: one 6-pdr, one 12-pdr, one 24-pounder, one 32-pdr, and four 68-pdrs. In addition to these, they also received some bronze guns: three 6-pdrs and one 12-pdr (all smoothbores), one rifled 4-pdr, and one 4-pdr howitzer.

# THE OPPOSING NAVIES

In the Paraguayan theater of operations, control of the main waterways was fundamental. The roads were few and of poor quality, and so rivers

The frigate *Amazonas*, flagship of the Imperial Brazilian Navy between 1864 and 1870. At the time of the Paraguayan War, this warship was the most formidable one in South America, on account of its heavy guns. The *Amazonas* was built by Wilson & Co. in Liverpool and entered service in 1851.

were the only practical means for commercial and long-distance travel. Rivers such as the Paraguay and Paraná are immense (certainly by European standards), providing both highways for military transport and formidable natural barriers to movement by land. Deep and wide, they were navigable by Brazil's ocean-going warships, but river movements were vulnerable to fire from shore batteries.

Paraguay's river fleet had been built up in the years before the war under the personal direction of both presidents López, to operate between the forts built along the major rivers. As the Triple Alliance would discover to its cost, the fleet strengthened Paraguay's ability to mount offensives. Nevertheless, the Paraguayan Navy had only two real warships: the steam corvettes *Tacuarí* and *Paraguarí* (620 and 730 tons respectively; each armed with two 68-pdr and six 32-pdr guns). Its 16 other large vessels were converted merchant ships: steamboats (displacing 150–650 tons, most armed with four 18-pdr guns) and *chatas* (towed wooden monitors, each with one heavy gun).

Brazil, by contrast, had more than 40 warships, with well-trained crews: the flagship was the 1,050-ton frigate *Amazonas* (one 70-pdr and five 68-pdr guns). The other warships of the Brazilian Navy included four steam corvettes (all 600-plus tons, with seven or eight 68-pdrs and 32-pdrs) and four gunboats (70–100 tons, each with between five and seven guns). Most of these vessels were stationed in the southern provinces of Brazil at the outbreak of war, but their commanders were accustomed to navigating deep into the interior—as far as Cuyabá in the Mato Grosso.

During its lengthy civil wars, Argentina did not have a navy, and thus the Paraguayan attack in 1865 found the country with just three warships; two of these were captured immediately when the Paraguayans occupied Corrientes. Numerous merchant vessels were used for transport and for providing logistical support to the Brazilians, but did not take part in any engagements.

A rudimentary Uruguayan Navy was organized in 1860. During the conflict, it deployed 18 vessels of various sizes (mainly transports) to support the Brazilian fleet, but once again these were not involved in combat.

# OPPOSING PLANS

## PARAGUAYAN

Francisco Solano López, knowing full well that the Brazilian Army's best units would be fighting in Uruguay against his *Blancos* allies, hoped to conduct a brief offensive war modeled on the lightning campaigns launched by Napoleon I across Europe. Paraguayan forces would be divided into two large columns: one attacking the province of Río Grande do Sul (to the east of Paraguay), and the other advancing on the province of Mato Grosso (to the north).

The Brazilian defense of the Amazonian province of Mato Grosso was patchy, since it was located on the extreme edges of the empire and was very difficult to reach by land. Troops and supplies had to be sent via riverine expeditions, and this caused significant logistical problems. As a result, the Paraguayans were confident their forces could occupy the province before the arrival of substantial Brazilian reinforcements.

The situation in Río Grande do Sul was different: this province was located just north of Uruguay and thus the Brazilian Army supporting Flores would need little time to relocate against the invaders approaching from the west. However, Francisco Solano López hoped to occupy the province as rapidly as possible in order to sever the overland supply lines of the Brazilian contingent fighting in Uruguay. After conquering Río Grande do Sul, the Paraguayans would be able to march south toward Uruguay: this way they could join forces with the Uruguayan *Blancos*, who were still holding out in their remaining strongholds.

Francisco Solano López had planned the war as a brief border conflict with Brazil, confident that the empire would prefer to relinquish two provinces than become involved in a large-scale conflict in the La Plata region; obviously, his predictions proved to be quite wrong. The Paraguayan dictator had misjudged the Uruguayan conservatives' military capabilities; in addition, he was convinced that the population of Río Grande do Sul would rise up in revolt against the Brazilian central government. The province had been independent for a decade (1835–45) under the guidance of local cattle magnates, but the harsh repression that followed the end of the secession had erased most of the local separatist ambitions.

Francisco Solano López made other mistakes in his planning: firstly, he was confident that Argentina would remain neutral in the conflict; and secondly, he felt sure that he could count on the external support of de Urquiza, the leader of the Argentine conservatives. Mitre's great rival still enjoyed strong support in his home provinces in the Argentine interior, and had a large number of ex-combatants under his personal control. As a result, López was sure that this internal threat would oblige Mitre to remain neutral; should Argentina intervene, he would encourage de Urquiza to launch a new federalist revolt.

When Argentina abandoned its neutrality, the Paraguayan plans dissolved into thin air. The war that Francisco Solano López hoped would be over in a few weeks soon transformed into a multinational conflict, which saw Paraguay fighting alone against an alliance of three countries.

## TRIPLE ALLIANCE

The Triple Alliance was not expecting a Paraguayan attack, and thus had not prepared any measures to counter Francisco Solano López's move. In 1864, all the future members of the alliance were experiencing serious military difficulties: the Brazilians were blocked in Uruguay, the Argentines were recovering from the last civil war, and Flores' Uruguayans were still an irregular army of revolutionaries. The situation only changed in 1865: the Brazilians assembled large numbers of reinforcements and sent them south, Mitre realized that Urquiza would not be joining Francisco Solano López, and the Uruguayans managed to extensively reorganize their armed forces.

The Paraguayans were well informed about the military capabilities of their enemies, and knew that the Argentines had recently demobilized most of their regular and National Guard units; this reassured them that Argentina would not represent a serious threat to their southern borders. In addition, Argentina lacked a proper navy and thus could not send troops north of the Paraná or against the formidable Fortress of Humaitá. The Argentines were also aware of these factors, and thus never planned an invasion of southern Paraguay; but everything changed when the Paraguayans launched their offensive and invaded the province of Corrientes. At that point, the Argentines were obliged to react, although they were in no state to threaten the Paraguayan defensive positions north of the Paraná.

After the Riachuelo, the supremacy of the Brazilian fleet enabled the Alliance to cross the large river and move against Paraguayan territory. In general, both Brazil and Argentina began the war with the objective of simply recovering their lost territories; very soon, however, they understood that Francisco Solano López and his new army were a threat that had to be neutralized in order to maintain the political equilibrium in the River Plate area. The subsequent invasion of Paraguay from the south would soon prove to be extremely challenging, due to the strong resistance put up by the enemy.

Flores' Uruguayans took part in the Paraguayan War with a relatively small number of troops, and only out of their political obligations toward Brazil and Argentina. Flores had relied heavily on his powerful allies to regain power and thus could not avoid involvement in Paraguay; moreover, Francisco Solano López would always pose a threat to the internal stability of Uruguay, due to his strong links with the *Blancos*.

A watercolor by Adolph Methfessel depicting the famous Paraguayan artillery piece called "El Criollo," aiming at Brazilian ironclads. El Criollo formed part of the Paraguayan defensive line of Angostura, which was built along the Paraná River. In order to produce this gun, all the bells from the churches of Asunción were melted down. El Criollo (a 150-pdr, weighing 4 tons) was captured by the Argentines and later melted down to create the statue of Christ the Redeemer of the Andes, erected at the La Cumbre Pass between Mendoza in Argentina and Santiago de Chile.

# THE CAMPAIGN

## BRAZIL INTERVENES IN URUGUAY, 1864

On September 6, 1864, some 18 months after Flores had launched his *Cruzada Libertadora* in Uruguay, Francisco Solano López sent a formal request to Mitre's government seeking clarification of the role played by Argentina in the new Uruguayan civil war. López feared, quite correctly, that the Argentines were supporting the revolutionary *Colorados* against his *Blancos* allies.

An Argentine gaucho photographed in Peru during 1866. Gauchos served in the Brazilian and Argentine armies as auxiliary light cavalry, acting as scouts and skirmishers.

Meanwhile, the Brazilians were preparing to intervene in Uruguay: after a last failed attempt to find a compromise between the two warring parties, on October 12, the Brazilian Army, under the command of General João de Deus Mena Barreto, crossed its southerly border with Uruguay. Initially, the Brazilians deployed just two divisions: the 1st Division (with two brigades of infantry and one brigade of cavalry), and the 2nd Division (two brigades of cavalry and the Horse Artillery Regiment) for a total of 6,000 men. This small, cavalry-dominated force initially met with no opposition from the *Blancos* and was able to join forces with Flores' revolutionary troops. The Brazilians had already deployed a powerful naval squadron in the River Plate, which consisted of one frigate and four gunboats: the latter would support the land forces in besieging the major enemy strongholds.

At this point, Francisco Solano López decided to intervene against Brazil. On November 12, the Brazilian ship *Marquês de Olinda*, which was sailing on the Paraguay River, was captured by the Paraguayan war-steamer *Tacuarí*. The Brazilian ship was carrying the new governor of Mato Grosso province and large amounts of weapons and ammunitions to the garrison of the Amazonian province. The Paraguayans seized its cargo and converted the vessel into a gunboat for their fleet. This effectively marked the opening of hostilities between Brazil and Paraguay, since both the Paraná and the Paraguay rivers were closed to Brazilian shipping. Francisco Solano López rapidly organized a division from the best military units stationed in Cerro León camp, and placed it under the command of Colonel Vicente Barrios; its mission was to invade the Brazilian province of Mato Grosso.

# PARAGUAY INVADES MATO GROSSO

The Paraguayan force (four infantry battalions, two cavalry squadrons, a regiment of artillery, and two companies of sappers) departed the capital Asunción on December 14, 1864, together with a large naval squadron. After sailing north on the Paraguay River, it joined forces with a division stationed in the north of the country (comprising two infantry battalions, six cavalry regiments, and an artillery battery). The Mato Grosso invasion force thus totaled around 8,000 soldiers. The majority of the Paraguayan force continued its movement along the river, but a special brigade was detached from the rest of the expedition and continued its movement overland.

The main obstacle for the Paraguayans was now the Brazilian fort of Nueva Coimbra, which was located on the river at a strategic point in the extreme south of Mato Grosso province. The defenders were few in number, but could count on the support of a steamer armed with six guns. Brazilian resistance at the fort proved to be stubborn and caused heavy losses among the Paraguayan attackers, but nevertheless, on December 30, 1864, they were forced to abandon their positions and left the guns and powder in the fort in the hands of the Paraguayans.

Over the course of the following weeks, the Paraguayans occupied all of southern Mato Grosso, meeting scarce resistance. The harsh terrain in the region then came into play, and the invaders experienced serious difficulties in continuing their advance. The decision was taken to call a halt, without having occupied the provincial capital Cuiabá. A force of 1,000 soldiers was left to garrison the newly conquered areas, while the rest of the expedition returned home.

While these events were taking place in Mato Grosso, the main body of the Brazilian Army continued to fight in Uruguay. Both Flores and his allies had moved against the strategic port of Paysandú, which was garrisoned by 1,200 *Blancos* with 15 guns. The defenders put up strong resistance, hoping that the Paraguayans would cross the border to help them. Siege operations commenced on December 6, 1864, with the Brazilian naval squadron and Horse Artillery Regiment bombarding Paysandú. On January 1, 1865, with the city almost entirely destroyed by bombardment, Paysandú was assaulted and taken by the troops under Flores' command.

With this key position now in their hands, the Brazilian–*Colorados* force could now march on the Uruguayan capital. To prevent a siege of Montevideo, the *Blancos* sent a column of 1,500 soldiers into the Brazilian province of Río Grande do Sul: the Uruguayan conservatives hoped that the Paraguayans would march eastward to join them, but at that point Francisco Solano López was not ready to make such a move. As a result, the small force of *Blancos* was defeated by the Brazilians, and withdrew to defend Montevideo. Resistance in the Uruguayan capital proved to be less stubborn than at Paysandú, and on February 22, 1865, after little fighting, the 14,000-strong Brazilian–*Colorados* force took the city. As head of the new provisional government, Flores now aligned his country with Brazil.

# THE PARAGUAYAN OCCUPATION OF CORRIENTES, 1865

Both Paraguay and Brazil were clearly preparing to fight for possession of Río Grande do Sul province. However, both sides would need permission from Mitre to cross the Argentine province of Misiones, which lay between Paraguay and Río Grande do Sul. Francisco Solano López had already assembled 20,000 men under command of General Wenceslao Robles on the border of Misiones, ready to invade. President Mitre, however, rejected the requests made by both countries.

López decided at this point to attack Argentina, with the goal of conquering the two northerly provinces of Misiones and Corrientes. He hoped that his attack on northern Argentina would encourage de Urquiza's Federalists to rise up against Mitre, but this did not materialize.

On April 13, 1865, a Paraguayan naval squadron of five steamers sailed down the Paraná and bombarded the city of Corrientes. Mitre had sent two of his three warships to protect the city, but these were attacked and then boarded by the Paraguayans; the ships were later incorporated into the Paraguayan Navy. After a light bombardment, Corrientes was occupied by General Robles without much resistance. The Paraguayans then left a garrison of 1,500 men in the captured city and advanced toward the south, in order to secure the rest of the province.

Buoyed by popular support in Buenos Aires province, Mitre was soon able to organize a response to the Paraguayan surprise attack: 2,000 soldiers, under the command of General Wenceslao Paunero, were sent north to oppose the enemy advance into Corrientes. At the same time, on May 1, 1865, Paraguay's enemies decided to coordinate their military efforts by signing the famous Treaty of the Triple Alliance: now Brazil, Argentina, and Uruguay were determined to fight to the bitter end to defeat Paraguay and Francisco Solano López.

On May 11, Robles' Paraguayans reached the Riachuelo River (a tributary of the Paraná), but were forced to stop by the presence of

Brazilian ships transporting materiel and reinforcements to the Argentine city of Corrientes. The Battle of the Riachuelo was fought in the waters opposite Corrientes, which had been captured for the second time by Paraguayan forces on May 26, 1865.

## Paraguay invades Río Grande do Sul, 1865

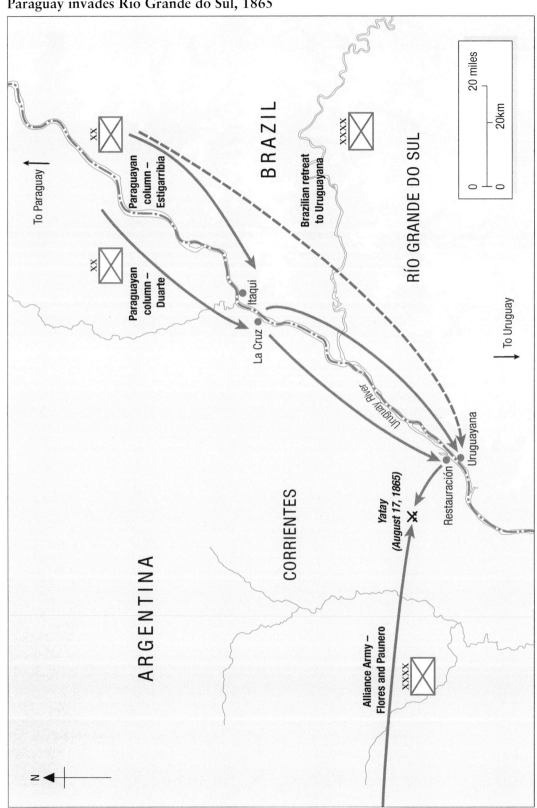

The Brazilian 1st Corpo de Voluntários da Pátria at the Battle of São Borja on June 10, 1865. This unit was formed at the Imperial Palace (Paço Imperial) in Rio de Janeiro from volunteers from various provinces of Brazil.

Paunero, awaiting them on the opposite bank. The Argentines had just four infantry battalions and a squadron of horse artillery, but were determined to repulse the Paraguayans. The presence of the powerful Brazilian naval squadron persuaded Robles to retreat, and he made no attempt to cross the Riachuelo.

At this point, Paunero embarked his troops on the Brazilian ships and sailed north toward Corrientes, intending to retake the city. On May 25, the Alliance forces began to bombard the Paraguayan defensive positions, and once Paunero's troops had disembarked, began an assault. The ensuing fight was extremely harsh and caused many losses on both sides; by the end of the day, Corrientes was back in Argentine hands. The following day, however, the Alliance commanders were informed that a large Paraguayan relief force was approaching Corrientes; this consisted of two infantry battalions and two cavalry regiments, far outnumbering Paunero's force. The Argentine soldiers re-embarked on the Brazilian ships and sailed down the river to avoid a direct confrontation with the superior Paraguayan force: as a result, Corrientes city was once again occupied by the Paraguayans.

While all these events were taking place in Corrientes, Francisco Solano López's troops had invaded Misiones province. His force, consisting of 12,000 men under the command of Colonel José Félix Estigarribia, comprised the following units: ten infantry battalions, six cavalry regiments, and an artillery battery with six guns. The Alliance forces in Misiones province were scarce, especially when compared to those of the invaders; as a result, the Paraguayan advance met very little resistance. On June 10, at San Borja, 1,000 defenders were attacked by Estigarribia: the Alliance troops were able to halt the Paraguayans for two days, but in the end the small city was conquered. San Borja controlled one of the main fords that could be used to cross the Uruguay River, which ran across

Misiones. Estigarribia continued his advance and forded the river, before marching across the whole Argentine province and taking control of it without any major engagements. By the beginning of August 1865, Misiones was under Paraguayan control and the soldiers of Francisco Solano López were ready to attack the Brazilians in Río Grande do Sul.

# THE BATTLE OF THE RIACHUELO, JUNE 11, 1865

Francisco Solano López had come to understand that the overall

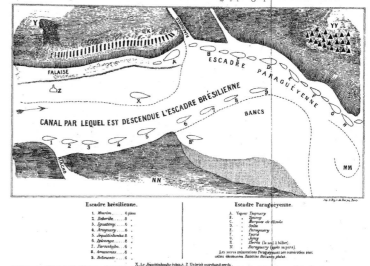

A French map of the Battle of the Riachuelo, showing the initial disposition of the Brazilian and Paraguayan fleets. The victory at the Riachuelo allowed the Brazilians to transport troops and supplies by water for the rest of the war, while blockading Paraguay's supply routes and contacts with the rest of the world.

superiority of the Brazilian fleet was a key factor in any Alliance victories; as a result, he planned to destroy the Brazilian warships. Both the Paraguayan Army and the Paraguayan Navy (commanded by Captain Pedro Ignacio Meza) would be involved in this. López would deploy a small land-based force at some distance upriver from the anchorage of the Brazilian fleet on the Paraná, with a battery of rifled 12-pdrs (the only one of its kind in the Paraguayan Army). Then, he would order his fleet to attack the Brazilian warships at daybreak while they were still anchored and their crews were on shore; the Paraguayan fleet was to slip past the enemy ships unnoticed, before turning back to attack them. The plan was to board the Brazilian warships, taking them by surprise, as any ship vs ship battle would see the Paraguayans destroyed by the enemy's superior naval artillery. If boarding was not possible, the Paraguayans would drive the Brazilians further up the river to isolate them from the rest of the Alliance forces and bring them under the fire of the battery of rifled guns.

**Order of battle, the Riachuelo, June 11, 1865**

| Brazilian | Paraguayan |
| --- | --- |
| *Amazonas* (wooden paddleship frigate) | *Taquarí* (ironclad paddleship corvette) |
| *Iguatemi* (wooden gunboat) | *Paraguarí* (wooden paddleship corvette) |
| *Parnaíba* (wooden corvette) | *Ygureí* (wooden paddleship) |
| *Araguarí* (wooden gunboat) | *Yporá* (wooden paddleship) |
| *Mearím* (wooden gunboat) | *Marquês de Olinda* (wooden paddleship) |
| *Jequitinhonha* (wooden paddleship corvette) | *Jejui* (wooden paddleship) |
| *Beberibe* (wooden paddleship corvette) | *Salto Guairá* (wooden paddleship) |
| *Belmonte* (wooden paddleship corvette) | *Pirabebé* (wooden paddleship) |
| *Ypiranga* (wooden gunboat) | Seven wooden gun batteries (*chatas*) |

Timing and stealth were the key factors in the success of this ambitious plan; the Paraguayans, however, experienced serious difficulties in coordination from the beginning of the operation. During the night of June 10/11, the Paraguayan fleet with eight warships and seven *chatas* (flat boats)

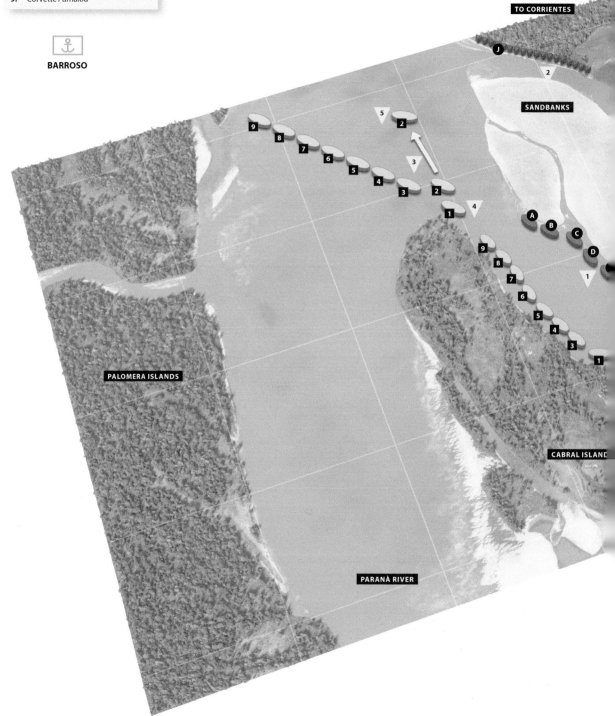

**BRAZILIAN FLEET**

1. Corvette *Belmonte*
2. Corvette *Jequitinhonha*
3. Frigate *Amazonas*
4. Corvette *Beberíbe*
5. Gunboat *Iguatemi*
6. Gunboat *Mearím*
7. Gunboat *Araguarí*
8. Gunboat *Ypiranga*
9. Corvette *Parnaíba*

**BARROSO**

TO CORRIENTES

SANDBANKS

PALOMERA ISLANDS

CABRAL ISLAND

PARANÀ RIVER

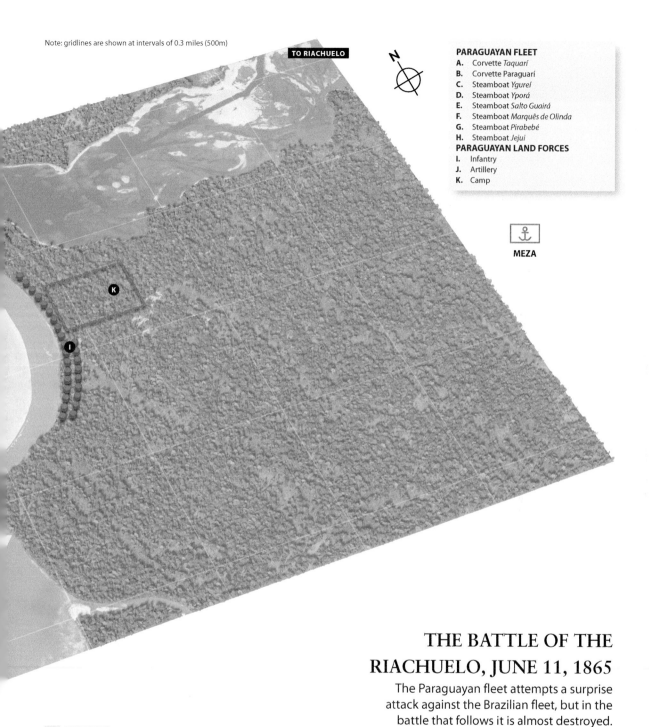

Note: gridlines are shown at intervals of 0.3 miles (500m)

TO RIACHUELO

N

**PARAGUAYAN FLEET**
A.  Corvette *Taquarí*
B.  Corvette Paraguarí
C.  Steamboat *Ygureí*
D.  Steamboat *Yporá*
E.  Steamboat *Salto Guairá*
F.  Steamboat *Marquês de Olinda*
G.  Steamboat *Pirabebé*
H.  Steamboat *Jejui*

**PARAGUAYAN LAND FORCES**
I.  Infantry
J.  Artillery
K.  Camp

MEZA

# THE BATTLE OF THE RIACHUELO, JUNE 11, 1865

The Paraguayan fleet attempts a surprise attack against the Brazilian fleet, but in the battle that follows it is almost destroyed.

## ▼ EVENTS

**1.** The Paraguayan fleet, after having left Humaitá during the night, sails across the Paraná River with the objective of boarding the Brazilian warships before sunrise. Due to technical problems, the Paraguayans reach the Brazilian fleet after several hours' delay. As a result, the Paraguayan commander Meza changes his plans and decides to continue down the river while firing against the docked Brazilian warships. The Brazilians respond to the fire accurately, and damage two enemy ships. At this point, the Paraguayans decide to turn upstream and anchor near the mouth of the Riachuelo Stream, in front of their camp.

**2.** Meanwhile, the Brazilians, led by Barroso, have started to pursue the Paraguayans. In doing so, however, they soon come under fire from the Paraguayan artillery and infantry on the shore.

**3.** The second ship in the Brazilian line, the corvette *Jequitinhonha*, inadvertently turns downstream and is followed by the whole fleet.

**4.** The first ship in the Brazilian line, the corvette *Belmonte*, is severely damaged after being isolated.

**5.** The *Jequitinhonha* is sunk by the Paraguayans, while the rest of the Brazilian fleet now sails upstream.

**6.** The damaged corvette *Belmonte* halts at Cabral Island. At this point, Barroso, who has escaped the Paraguayan trap, decides to turn against the anchored enemy ships in order to prevent their escape. The ensuing clash is a complete disaster for Meza, who loses numerous warships.

The Battle of the Riachuelo, fought on the Paraná River on June 11, 1865. In the central part of this picture is the commander of the victorious Brazilians, Francisco Manuel Barroso da Silva, on the flagship of the Brazilian fleet the paddle steamer frigate *Amazonas*.

departed from its main naval base of Humaitá; as it sailed downriver toward the Brazilian fleet, however, the *Yporá* broke down, causing a serious delay for the Paraguayans. As a result, Meza's fleet reached the anchored Brazilian warships when the sun was already high in the sky.

The Brazilian ships were deployed in line on a bend in the river, where the Paraná was divided into several smaller channels by eight islands of differing size and shape. The sudden appearance of the Paraguayans took the Brazilians by surprise and caused some initial panic; Meza, due to the delay, was obliged to change his plans and thus decided to begin bombarding the enemy warships while continuing to sail down the river. The fire of the Paraguayans had little effect on the Brazilian ships, while the response of the Brazilians was accurate: the *Jejui* and one *chata* were soon put out of action. At this point, Meza decided to turn around and retreat, in order to benefit from the protective fire of the land battery near the Paraguayan camp. Having sailed back upriver, his warships anchored at the mouth of the Riachuelo.

The Brazilians had no idea that a trap had been set for them by the Paraguayans, and thus launched a close pursuit of Meza's retreating warships. As they came within range of the Paraguayan fleet and rifled guns, the first Brazilian ship in the attacking line, the *Belmonte*, was soon put out of action. The second, the *Jequitinhonha*, inadvertently turned downstream, ran aground on a sandbank, and was then sunk by the Paraguayans.

The two fleets then closed to contact, and the Paraguayans attempted to board the Brazilian warships. The attackers almost managed to board the *Parnaíba*, but were repulsed by the other Brazilian ships. After more than four hours of harsh close combat, the surviving Paraguayan warships decided to abandon their positions and sailed upriver toward Humaitá.

The clash was a disaster for the Paraguayan Navy: the *Paraguarí*, *Marquês de Olinda*, *Jejui*, *Salto Guairá*, and all the *chatas* were lost. The Brazilians, instead, suffered only one loss—the *Jequitinhonha*; the damage to the *Belmonte* was repairable. The Alliance fleet, fearing that the Paraguayans might have prepared other traps upriver, returned to its starting position; this was a mistake, because at least two of the surviving Paraguayan warships were so badly damaged that they could easily have been sunk.

A few months after the battle, the Brazilian fleet returned to Corrientes, since it was in no condition to attack the fortress of Humaitá. The Alliance retreat, however, was harrassed by Paraguayan land forces and their rifled battery, which followed them along the banks of the river and bombarded them on two separate occasions, inflicting numerous casualties on the Brazilians.

# YATAY AND URUGUAYANA, AUGUST–SEPTEMBER, 1865

On August 6, 1865, the forces under Estigarribia captured the key Brazilian town of Uruguayana, which was located on the border between Misiones and Río Grande do Sul. Despite being garrisoned by 8,000 soldiers, it was easily taken by the Paraguayans. At this point, it seemed that Estigarribia was ready to push deep into Río Grande do Sul province, exactly as he had done in Misiones; however, the Alliance had by now been able to assemble a large army of 16,000 soldiers in the region, and it was already heading for Uruguayana. The vanguard of this force, led by Flores, reached the Paraguayan positions at Yatay on August 17.

In the ensuing battle, the Paraguayans (a vanguard of 3,200 men under the command of Colonel Pedro Duarte) were attacked and defeated by Flores' 10,500-strong spearhead. The clash began with a Paraguayan charge against the Uruguayan infantry, commanded by de Pallejas; the assault was repulsed after some fierce fighting, which both sides taking extensive casualties. Much of the battlefield was waterlogged, since the adjacent Yatay and Uruguay rivers had flooded over the previous days, and this hindered the Paraguayan advance. After stopping the enemy, the Alliance troops launched a cavalry counterattack that proved highly effective, and pushed the Paraguayans back to their starting positions. In the final phase of the battle, the Alliance cavalry was able to partially encircle the retreating Paraguayan infantry and attack it from the rear. The Alliance suffered 300 casualties, while the Paraguayans counted 1,700 killed and 1,200 captured. The Uruguayans played a prominent role in this clash, with their veterans showing particular courage in the fight; the Brazilians and the Argentines played secondary roles in this battle.

The Alliance was now free to advance on Uruguayana, in order to retake the city. The latter was well garrisoned by the Paraguayans, being located in a strategic position on the Uruguay River. While the Alliance troops were fighting at Yatay against the Paraguayans, Estigarribia significantly improved the city's defenses, and with 8,000 soldiers under him, was determined to defend the

The Voluntários da Pátria assaulting the Paraguayan positions at the Battle of Yatay, August 17, 1865.

An engraving showing the Paraguayan surrender of Uruguayana (September 18, 1865) to the Emperor of Brazil, Pedro II (the central figure on the horse, wearing the traditional gaucho costume of Río Grande do Sul province with poncho and slouch hat).

city for as long as possible. The Alliance troops, however, were well prepared for an attack on the Paraguayan positions: their forces had been organized into three corps (I Uruguayan, II Argentine, and III Brazilian), and now numbered in the region of 18,000 men, supported by 42 artillery guns.

The Alliance, however, opted to besiege Uruguayana and did not launch a major attack on the city; it was clear that the defenders would soon run out of supplies. Both the Brazilian emperor Pedro II and the Argentine president Mitre personally joined the Alliance besieging forces, thus giving a high symbolic value to the reconquest of the Brazilian city on the Uruguay River. On September 4, Estigarribia rejected a first Alliance request to surrender, but four days later (on September 18), he was obliged to give in, due to the worsening conditions in which his men found themselves (2,500 of them had already died from hunger and sickness during the brief siege).

With the fall of Uruguayana, the initial phase of the war, which was marked by Paraguayan expansion efforts, came to an end. The Brazilian province of Río Grande do Sul was now free from any threat. After the major defeats at the Riachuelo and Uruguayana, Francisco Solano López realized that his dispersed military forces needed to be drawn back in, in order to defend Paraguayan national territory. As a result, all Paraguayan forces in Corrientes crossed the Paraguay River and headed back to the north.

# THE ALLIANCE ADVANCE ON PARAGUAY, 1866

By the end of 1865, the Paraguayans had withdrawn from the Brazilian and Argentine territories that they had previously conquered, with the exception of southern Mato Grosso. López's expansionist dreams had been destroyed by the reality of a war that had now transformed itself into a continental conflict. Both of the warring sides now needed to evaluate the military situation carefully and take some key decisions.

Paraguay had lost most of its fleet and a large number of troops, but could still count on a vast manpower reserve and on the strong defenses that protected the southern part of its national territory. Continuing the war meant defending the homeland from foreign aggression, but the Paraguayans were confident that they could repulse any invading Alliance force and inflict heavy losses on it. A critical factor in this confidence was the

Another depiction of the Paraguayan surrender at Uruguayana. Most of the captured Paraguayan soldiers were obliged to enlist in the Alliance Army, thus forming the Paraguayan Legion and the Independencia Battalion.

# Retaking Río Grande do Sul and Corrientes

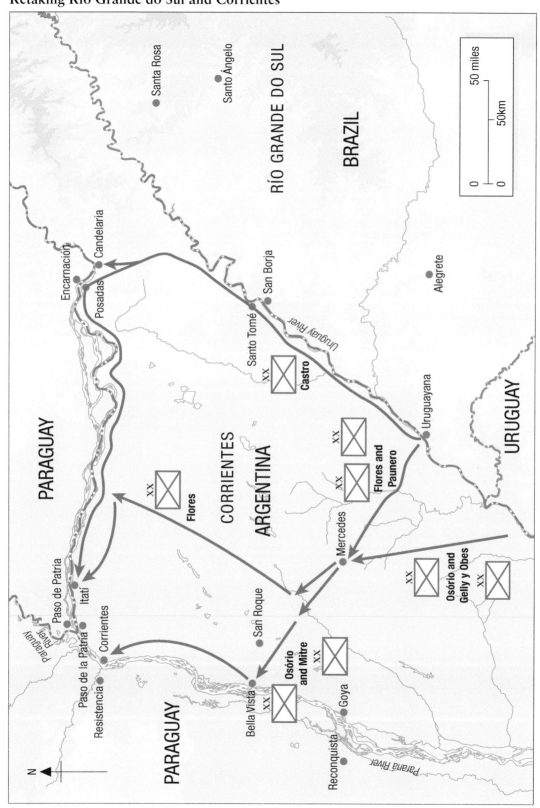

A bird's-eye-view of the Paraguayan War's main theater of operations. The Paraguay River divides the inhospitable region of the Chaco from the populated areas of Paraguay. To the south is the main Alliance camp of Tuyutí. Moving north along the river are the Paraguayan defensive positions of Curuzú and Curupaytí; the latter is located just south of the Fortress of Humaitá. This image allows us to understand how complex and massive the Paraguayan defensive system was and why it took such a long time for the Alliance to conquer it. Since deficiencies in reconnaissance had been among the most important causes of the Alliance defeat at Curupaytí, after this battle Caxias ordered the creation of a new Balloon Corps for observation of the enemy positions—the first in South America's military history.

impressive Fortress of Humaitá, along with the other defensive positions protecting the border with Argentina.

For the Alliance, the situation was more complex. Argentina had serious internal problems, and thus would have preferred to end the war without invading Paraguay. The Indians of Patagonia were in revolt, and Argentine public opinion was mostly satisfied with the reconquest of Corrientes and Misiones. Moreover, de Urquiza had formally expressed his opposition to any eventual prosecution of the hostilities. Mitre feared that a prolonged mobilization could lead to revolt in the interior provinces, which were under the control of the Federalist leader. In Uruguay, the situation was similar: the country was still recovering from its civil war and the *Blancos* were doing their best to oppose their country's participation in the conflict against Paraguay. Only Brazil, among the Triple Alliance, clearly intended to continue the war against Francisco Solano López. Pedro II had understood that Paraguay (more particularly, the formidable army that López had organized) represented a serious threat to any Brazilian presence on the River Plate. Both the Paraguayan dictator and his military forces had to be defeated if the political equilibrium in the region was to be restored.

Following negotiations between the Alliance powers, Argentina and Uruguay agreed to continue the war alongside their more powerful ally, and plans were formed for an invasion of Paraguay. The Alliance invasion force was gradually assembled at Paso de la Patria, located 25 miles northeast of Corrientes on the Argentine side of the Paraná River, facing the Paraguayan Paso de Patria village. The ford that was located between them was the best place for a large army to cross the Paraná on its way to invading Paraguay.

In December 1865, having assumed overall command of all Paraguayan forces, Francisco Solano López assembled a large force at Paso de Patria and built an immense encampment there. The Paraguayan camp was built above a vast area that was covered in deep lagoons and muddy terrain, intersected by impenetrable tropical jungle or by swamps thick with high grass. The camp used advantageous terrain features, being located between two large lagoons that covered its flanks, and was protected by more than 30 guns emplaced along the trenches dug around its perimeter. In total, the Paraguayans gathered at the camp numbered around 30,000.

Despite being outnumbered by the Alliance forces, the Paraguayans had no intention of remaining on the defensive. López soon started to harass the Triple Alliance positions by sending small raiding parties across the river on canoes. These attacks, conducted by small groups of Paraguayans numbering a few hundred or so, took place almost daily and inflicted considerable damage on the Alliance forces. These raids continued for three months, with the Alliance unable to provide an effective response. The Argentine pickets around Paso de la Patria suffered the most. For these raiding operations, the Paraguayan logistical base was the fort of Itapirú, which was located opposite Paso de la Patria and near to their camp at Paso de Patria.

On January 31, 1866, López launched the largest of his assaults against Paso de la Patria, which soon transformed into a small battle. A total of 1,200 Paraguayans supported by Congreve rocket-launchers were sent against the Argentine positions, with orders to join forces with another Paraguayan storming party that had been sent to the same area a few days before. The new Paraguayan raid was more ambitious than any of the previous ones: López wanted to establish a defensive position on the southern bank of the river, in view of a possible large-scale attack on the Alliance camp. The sector attacked by the Paraguayans was under Argentine control, and had been targeted during many of the previous raids. Fortunately for the Alliance troops, Mitre had reinforced the area by sending an additional division (comprising the National Guard units of Buenos Aires) to bolster the defense. Initially, the Paraguayans were able to occupy Paso de la Patria, but soon the Argentines managed to organize a counterattack, and caught the attackers by surprise as they were digging trenches to protect their new positions. After some brutal close-quarter fighting, the Paraguayans were hit hard twice on their flanks, and were forced to retreat to the fort of Itapirú.

Over the following weeks, the Paraguayans continued to conduct raiding operations, but this time López targeted the Uruguayan Vanguard Division, which was based at the village of Itatí, located on the southern bank of the river 25 miles east of Paso de la Patria. López ordered three of his remaining steamers stationed at Humaitá to sail down the Paraná, with orders to stop at Paso de Patria and embark a special assault force comprising two infantry battalions, two artillery guns, and two rocket-launchers. This small force's mission was to attack Itatí. The Paraguayan attack took the Uruguayans by surprise; because Flores was not present in the village at the time, the Vanguard Division opted to avoid a direct confrontation and abandoned Itatí. The Paraguayans looted and burned both the village of Itatí and the Triple Alliance camp there, but then re-embarked on their ships and returned to Paso de Patria.

A Brazilian corporal of the 1st Corpo de Voluntários da Pátria in 1865. Note the Corpo de Voluntários da Pátria badge and rank stripes on his left sleeve.

A Brazilian cavalry officer (left) with a captured Paraguayan soldier (right).

In March 1866, the Alliance finally decided to respond to these Paraguayan offensive actions, making use of the superiority of the Brazilian fleet. On March 21, the Brazilian warships arrived at Paso de la Patria and prepared themselves for an attack against the Paraguayan fort of Itapirú. The destruction of the latter would halt any further Paraguayan raiding, and would also be crucial for any future Alliance crossing of the Paraná at Paso de Patria. The Paraguayan defences of Itapirú were reinforced by the presence of the warship *Gualeguay*, which had remained in the area after the February raid against Itatí. It was supported by two wooden *chatas*, which could be maneuvered close to the Brazilian ships by the *Gualeguay* before opening fire with their mounted guns.

The first *chata* was brought near the Brazilian fleet on March 22; having fired its guns, it was targeted by three Alliance ironclads and destroyed before causing any serious damage to the Brazilian ships. The second *chata* was towed near the Alliance positions on March 27, and had better fortune than the first: it managed to hit and severely damage an ironclad. At this point the Alliance commanders, who had probably underestimated the threat posed by the *chata*, sent three ironclads and four wooden steamers to destroy it. At the end of the clash, despite suffering some significant damage, the Brazilian ships were able to put the *chata* out of action. The Brazilians now focused on sinking the *Gualeguay* before moving against the fort of Itapirú; the latter, however, was by now only defended by a single gun, and thus did not represent a serious threat to the Alliance. The *Gualeguay* proved to be a much tougher opponent for the Brazilians, and was able to resist alone for almost three weeks, throughout which it continued to act aggressively. Each day, it sailed close to the Alliance positions and opened fire; when the Brazilian ships moved to respond, *Gualeguay* managed to retreat without being intercepted or severely damaged.

During these three weeks, the Alliance bombarded the fort of Itapirú, both with their warships and with a land battery that was placed at Paso de la Patria for this specific purpose (the latter comprising 12 rifled 12-pdr guns and four 13in. mortars). Unable to sink the *Gualeguay*, the Brazilians opted to move against Itapirú all the same: on April 5, they landed a token force of 900 men on the Cerrito, a sandbank located in the middle of the Paraná near to the fort of Itapirú. The Brazilians fortified the newly conquered position and prepared themselves for a final effort against the Paraguayan fort. López sent 800 soldiers to retake the Cerrito, organizing a night attack with canoes: this, however, ended in failure and cost the Paraguayans 500 casualties.

By mid-April, the Triple Alliance was ready to cross the Paraná and invade Paraguayan territory. The force assembled to cross the river, under the overall command of the Brazilian Marshal Manuel Luís Osório, comprised a total of 14,365 soldiers: 9,465 Brazilians, 4,000 Argentines, and 900 Uruguayans. The crossing would be supported by the Brazilian fleet, divided into three divisions: the 1st Division would bombard the fort of Itapirú, the 2nd Division would target the Paraguayan camp of Paso de Patria, and the 3rd Division would escort the transport ships during the crossing.

On April 16, the operation began. Although difficulties were foreseen, everything went according to plan and the Paraguayans made no attempt to oppose the Alliance landings on their side of the river. The Brazilians soon fortified their new positions by digging trenches and by deploying their artillery; at the same time, they started to advance toward Itapirú with the objective of taking the fort.

On April 17, after further Alliance troops had crossed the river during the night, the Paraguayans launched a counterattack against the advancing enemy: this, however, was conducted with only 1,600 troops and had little impact on the Alliance positions. López understood the gravity of the situation; he ordered the Itapirú garrison to abandon the fort (there was little hope of defending it successfully) and sent 1,800 reinforcements to aid the 1,600 soldiers involved in the counterattack. This new effort, however, was also repulsed with heavy losses for the Paraguayans. At the same point, the Brazilians entered the fort of Itapirú: now, the Alliance crossing of the Paraná could continue unhindered. López now decided to order most of his remaining 24,000 soldiers to abandon the encampment at Paso de Patria, aware that it would soon come under fire from the Brazilian warships. In order to cover his retreat, López left a small stay-behind force and some artillery pieces in the camp.

On April 20, the Alliance began to invest the Paraguayan camp, and bombarded it for two days. The main body of López's force had moved to a new, much more secure defensive position, located behind the vast marsh of Estero Bellaco, with the Paraguay River on one side and the Paraná River on the other. López now ordered the few remaining Paraguayan defenders to raise Paso de Patria camp to the ground before abandoning it. In recent days, the *Gualeguay* had also left Paso de Patria and retreated back to Humaitá.

Over the following two weeks, both armies paused to reorganize. The Alliance completed the transportation of all its units across the river, while the Paraguayans fortified their new camp at Estero Bellaco.

# THE BATTLE OF ESTERO BELLACO, MAY 2, 1866

A Triple Alliance vanguard (comprising four Uruguayan and six Brazilian infantry battalions, two artillery batteries, and a Brazilian cavalry regiment, all under the command of Flores) soon moved against López's new encampment at Estero Bellaco. However, Flores approached the Paraguayan positions without adequately considering the terrain, and encamped his Vanguard Division just south of the Estero Bellaco marsh. Flores' main objective at the head of the vanguard was to tie down the Paraguayans while the main body of the Alliance Army built a new entrenched camp at Paso de la Patria.

On May 2, Francisco Solano López sent a force of 4,500 infantrymen, 1,000 cavalrymen, and an artillery battery against the Alliance vanguard. The Paraguayan attacking force was divided into three columns, which crossed the Estero Bellaco marsh following three different routes. Flores' men were taken completely by surprise: all their artillery was captured and the four Uruguayan infantry battalions under his command had to fight

## THE BATTLE OF ESTERO BELLACO, MAY 2, 1866 (PP. 52–53)

After crossing the Paraná, the main objective of Flores' division was to pin down the Paraguayans while most of the Alliance Army built a new entrenched camp at Paso de Patria to the south. On May 2, Francisco Solano López sent a force of 4,500 infantrymen and 1,000 cavalrymen with one battery against the Alliance vanguard.

This illustration shows the Paraguayan infantry attacking the Uruguayan soldiers in the Vanguard Division, in particular the line infantry battalion *24 de Abril*. The latter, together with the Florida Battalion, was one of the Uruguayan contingent's best units. The Uruguayans formed a defensive square and were able to inflict heavy losses on the attackers.

The Paraguayan infantrymen (**1**) are dressed in their customary red shirts and shakos, and are armed with flintlock muskets. The officers (**2**) are dressed in dark blue and had revolvers. The infantrymen of the *24 de Abril* Battalion (**3**) are in white uniforms, with dark blue kepis; their officers' uniforms (**4**) are clearly French in style. The Uruguayans had the advantage of being armed with percussion muskets.

The Uruguayan infantry battalions had to fight with enormous courage to maintain their positions. Flores' units remained isolated for several hours and suffered high numbers of casualties before the main Alliance Army moved from Paso de Patria to help them.

with enormous courage to maintain their positions. Flores' men remained isolated for several hours and suffered high losses before elements of the main Alliance force moved from Paso de Patria to support them.

At the end of the day, when the Paraguayans returned to their starting positions, it soon became clear that the Battle of Estero Bellaco had resulted in a futile massacre for both sides. Alliance losses consisted of 400 Uruguayans, 311 Brazilians, and 61 Argentines. In addition, 700 Paraguayan prisoners, who had been incorporated into the Vanguard Division after being captured at Yatay and Uruguayana, had deserted and rejoined their former comrades. After Estero Bellaco, the Uruguayan presence in the Vanguard Division was strongly reduced due to the losses suffered, and its ranks were filled with Argentine soldiers. The Paraguayans lost 2,300 soldiers in the battle.

On May 23, 1866, having reorganized its forces, the Alliance began advancing toward López's positions north of Estero Bellaco. In total, the number of Alliance troops amounted to 32,000, an impressive figure for South American standards of the time. The advancing army was under the overall command of Mitre, who had already commanded large contingents in pitched battles on two occasions during the Argentine civil wars. The advance took place in three columns, and halted only after reaching the northerly point of the Estero Bellaco marsh.

The Alliance front-line positions took the form of a horseshoe and were easily defensible. To reinforce their positions, a trench was dug around its new camp and two redoubts were constructed on the front line, one in the center and one on the left flank. The redoubts and trench lines were protected by 150 field guns. The site where the Alliance built this camp was known as Tuyutí, and was located a mile to the north of Paso de Patria.

On May 25, knowing that the Alliance was about to advance against his positions, López decided to launch a massive attack on the enemy's new camp, in order to destroy it. The ensuing battle would be decisive for the course of the war, since both sides would engage all their available military resources. Against the Alliance's 32,000 soldiers, López's Paraguayans numbered 24,000.

# ORDER OF BATTLE, TUYUTÍ

## PARAGUAY

### 1ST ATTACKING COLUMN (3,500 MEN)

Commander: General Vicente Barrios
6 infantry battalions
2 cavalry regiments
4 rocket-launchers, and several light artillery guns

### 2ND ATTACKING COLUMN (6,300 MEN)

Commander: Brigadier-General Isidoro Resquín
2 infantry battalions
8 cavalry regiments
2 rocket-launchers

### 3RD ATTACKING COLUMN (5,000 MEN)

Commander: Colonel José Díaz
5 infantry battalions
2 cavalry regiments
4 light artillery guns

### 4TH ATTACKING COLUMN (4,200 MEN)

Commander: Colonel Hilario Marcó
4 infantry battalions
2 cavalry regiments

### RESERVE (6,000 MEN)

Commander: Colonel José Bruguéz
Unspecified units, including 2 horse artillery regiments

## TRIPLE ALLIANCE

### BRAZIL

**1st Division**
Commander: General Francisco Argolo
8th Brigade
Commander: Colonel José
    8th Infantry Battalion
    16th Infantry Battalion
    10th Corpo de Voluntários da Pátria Battalion

46th Corpo de Voluntários da Pátria Battalion
10th Brigade
Commander: Colonel Carlos Resín
    2nd Infantry Battalion
    13th Infantry Battalion
    22nd Corpo de Voluntários da Pátria Battalion
    26th Corpo de Voluntários da Pátria Battalion
    40th Corpo de Voluntários da Pátria Battalion
**3rd Division**
Commander: General Antônio de Sampaio
5th Brigade
Commander: Colonel Belo
    3rd Infantry Battalion
    4th Infantry Battalion
    6th Infantry Battalion
    4th Corpo de Voluntários da Pátria Battalion
7th Brigade
Commander: Colonel Fernando Machado
    1st Infantry Battalion
    6th Corpo de Voluntários da Pátria Battalion
    9th Corpo de Voluntários da Pátria Battalion
    11th Corpo de Voluntários da Pátria Battalion
**4th Division**
Commander: General Manuel Marques de Sousa
11th Brigade
Commander: Colonel José Autó
    10th Infantry Battalion
    14th Infantry Battalion
    20th Corpo de Voluntários da Pátria Battalion
    31st Corpo de Voluntários da Pátria Battalion
13th Brigade
Commander: Lieutenant-Colonel C. Pereira
    12th Infantry Battalion
    1st Corpo de Voluntários da Pátria Battalion
    19th Corpo de Voluntários da Pátria Battalion
    24th Corpo de Voluntários da Pátria Battalion
**6th Division**
Commander: General Vitorino Monteiro
12th Brigade
Commander: Colonel Joaquin Coelho Kelly
    5th Infantry Battalion
    7th Infantry Battalion
    3rd Corpo de Voluntários da Pátria Battalion
    16th Corpo de Voluntários da Pátria Battalion
14th Brigade
Commander: Lieutenant-Colonel Jerónimo dos Reis Salustiano
    2nd Infantry Battalion
    14th Corpo de Voluntários da Pátria Battalion
    21st Corpo de Voluntários da Pátria Battalion
    30th Corpo de Voluntários da Pátria Battalion
18th Brigade
Commander: Colonel E. Silva
    38th Corpo de Voluntários da Pátria Battalion
    41st Corpo de Voluntários da Pátria Battalion
    51st Corpo de Voluntários da Pátria Battalion
**2nd Cavalry Division**
Commander: General Mena Barreto
1st Brigade
Commander: Lieutenant-Colonel Augusto de Araujo Bastos
    2nd Cavalry Regiment
    3rd Cavalry Regiment
    I National Guard Cavalry Corps
4th Brigade
Commander: Lieutenant-Colonel Manoel de Oliveira Bueno
    II National Guard Cavalry Corps
    V National Guard Cavalry Corps
    VII National Guard Cavalry Corps
**5th Cavalry Division**
Commander: Colonel T. Pinho
3rd Brigade

Commander: Lieutenant-Colonel Julio Mesquita
    IV National Guard Cavalry Corps
    VI National Guard Cavalry Corps
    XI National Guard Cavalry Corps
15th Brigade
Commander: Colonel Demetro Ribeiro
    III National Guard Cavalry Corps
    IX National Guard Cavalry Corps
    X National Guard Cavalry Corps
**Volunteer Cavalry Brigade**
Commander: Brigadier-General Antonio de Sousa Neto
1st Volunteer Cavalry
2nd Volunteer Cavalry
3rd Volunteer Cavalry
4th Volunteer Cavalry
**Artillery Train**
Commander: General Andrea
**17th Brigade**
Commander: Colonel Hilario Gurjão
1st Mounted Artillery Regiment
1st Foot Artillery Battalion
3rd Foot Artillery Battalion
**19th Brigade**
Commander: Colonel Francisco Gomes de Freitas
Engineer Battalion
7th Corpo de Voluntários da Pátria Battalion
42nd Corpo de Voluntários da Pátria Battalion

## ARGENTINA

**I Army Corps**
Commander: General Wenceslao Paunero
1st Division
Commander: Colonel Ignacio Rivas
    1st Brigade
    Commander: Lieutenant-Colonel Manuel Rosetti
        1st Infantry Battalion
        5th Infantry Battalion
    2nd Brigade
    Commander: Lieutenant-Colonel Juan Bautista Charlone
        Legión Militár Infantry Battalion
2nd Division
Commander: Colonel José Arredondo
    3rd Brigade
    Commander: Lieutenant-Colonel Manuel Fraga
        4th Infantry Battalion
        6th Infantry Battalion
    4th Brigade
    Commander: Lieutenant-Colonel Orms
        2nd Infantry Battalion
        1st Legion of Volunteers
3rd Division
Commander: Colonel José Ramón Esquivel
    5th Brigade
    Commander: Colonel José Ramón Esquivel
        National Guard Infantry Battalion Corrientes
        National Guard Infantry Battalion Rosario
    6th Brigade
    Commander: Lieutenant-Colonel Casanova
        National Guard Infantry Battalion Catamarca
        National Guard Infantry Battalion Tucumán
4th Division
Commander: Colonel Mateo Martinez
    7th Brigade
    Commander: Lieutenant-Colonel Adolfo Orma
        3rd Infantry Battalion
        2nd Legion of Volunteers
    8th Brigade
    Commander: Lieutenant-Colonel Benjamin Calvete
        National Guard Infantry Battalion Santa Fé
        National Guard Infantry Battalion Salta

Cavalry Brigade
Commander: Colonel José Maria Fernandes
    Mitre's Mounted Escort
    1st Cavalry Regiment
    National Guard Cavalry Regiment of Santa Fé
Artillery Brigade
Commander: Lieutenant-Colonel Leopoldo Nelson
    2nd Horse Artillery Battery
    3rd Horse Artillery Battery
    4th Horse Artillery Battery
**II Army Corps**
Commander: General Juan Andrés Gelly y Obes
1st Division
Commander: General Emilio Conesa
    1st National Guard Infantry Battalion of Buenos Aires
    2nd National Guard Infantry Battalion of Buenos Aires
    3rd National Guard Infantry Battalion of Buenos Aires
    4th National Guard Infantry Battalion of Buenos Aires
2nd Division
Commander: Colonel José Bustillos
    5th National Guard Infantry Battalion of Buenos Aires
    6th National Guard Infantry Battalion of Buenos Aires
    7th National Guard Infantry Battalion of Buenos Aires
    8th National Guard Infantry Battalion of Buenos Aires
3rd Division
Commander: Colonel Julio de Vedia
    National Guard Infantry Battalion Córdoba
    National Guard Infantry Battalion San Juán
    National Guard Infantry Battalion Segundo de Entre Ríos
    National Guard Infantry Battalion Mendoza
4th Division

Commander: Colonel Mateo Martínez
    9th Infantry Battalion
    12th Infantry Battalion
    National Guard Infantry Battalion Tercero de Entre Ríos
    National Guard Infantry Battalion La Rioja
Cavalry Division
Commander: Colonel Oryazabal
    1st National Guard Cavalry Regiment of Buenos Aires
    2nd National Guard Cavalry Regiment of Buenos Aires
Artillery Section
Commander: Colonel Federico Mitre
    1st Horse Artillery Battery

### URUGUAY

**Uruguayan Division**
Commander: General Venancio Flores
**1st Infantry Brigade**
Commander: Colonel León de Pallejas
Infantry Battalion Florida
Infantry Battalion 24 de Abril
**2nd Infantry Brigade**
Commander: Lieutenant-Colonel Marcelino Castro
Infantry Battalion Voluntários de la Libertad
Infantry Battalion Independencia
**Cavalry Brigade**
Commander: Colonel de Castro
1st National Guard Cavalry Regiment
2nd National Guard Cavalry Regiment
4th National Guard Cavalry Regiment
**Artillery Section**

# THE FIRST BATTLE OF TUYUTÍ, MAY 24, 1866

The Battle of Tuyutí has been called many things, including "the South-American Waterloo," due to the fact that the Paraguayans launched several fruitless cavalry charges against the Alliance infantry squares. From a purely numerical point of view, it was the largest pitched battle ever fought in South America to date, and resulted in more casualties in a single day than any other battle on the continent.

A grainy photograph of Uruguayan officers and soldiers of the Battalion "24 de April," waiting in their trenches during the First Battle of Tuyutí, May 24, 1866.

Francisco Solano López divided his forces into four columns. The 1st, under General Barrios, was to attack the Alliance left flank with 3,000 infantrymen and 500 cavalrymen; the 2nd, under General Resquín, was to advance against the Alliance right flank with 2,000 infantrymen and 4,000 cavalrymen; and the 3rd, under Colonel Díaz, and the 4th under Colonel Marcó, were to attack the Alliance center with 6,000 infantrymen and 3,000 cavalrymen. A reserve of around 6,000 soldiers remained in the Paraguayan camp, with most of the artillery (around 50 field pieces). The four columns were to take the Alliance camp by surprise, attacking simultaneously. The plan was for the Paraguayans' superior cavalry to spread panic among the Alliance infantrymen before they could organize themselves for the defense.

## THE FIRST BATTLE OF TUYUTÍ, MAY 24, 1866 (PP. 58–59)

At Tuyutí, López divided his attacking force into four columns: the 1st under Barrios, the 2nd under Resquín, the 3rd under Díaz, and the 4th under Marcó. Barrios' column attacked the Brazilians on the left of the Alliance Army, where the defenders had built a strong redoubt known as Fosso de Mallet. Barrios had some initial success against the enemy infantry, and the Paraguayans almost reached the Alliance tents before being repulsed by a Brazilian cavalry counterattack.

This illustration depicts the moment of the counterattack, with the Brazilian cavalry charging the Paraguayans in order to halt their advance. The Paraguayan cavalrymen (**1**), dressed in red shirts and shakos, are armed with lances and sabers; most

of them also have the famous, lethal *bolas* (**2**), which were used to entangle the legs of enemy horses. The Brazilian regular cavalrymen (**3**) wear the simple, dark blue campaign uniform, which was worn together with white trousers and kepi covers during hot months. All the Brazilian horsemen are armed with sabers; those equipped with carbines (**4**) do not carry a lance.

By 4.30 p.m., the Battle of Tuyutí was over: the Alliance soldiers had been able to defend their camp and the remnants of the attacking Paraguayans were retreating back to their positions. The Paraguayans lost 6,000 soldiers, the Alliance 1,000. López's assault against the Alliance camp had been a disaster: he had lost most of his best men, especially from the cavalry.

As previously, the Paraguayan dictator's ambitious plans required perfect coordination and timing to be effective. The first attacking column to advance was that of Barrios, since it had to cross difficult, marshy terrain. The Paraguayans faced numerous challenges during their advance: the cavalry had to dismount, and the infantry could only move forward slowly. Barrios reached the positions assigned to him three hours behind schedule, during which the other columns had to await his arrival (they had been much faster in reaching their starting positions). During the long wait, the Paraguayans were spotted by Alliance scouts, who returned to their camp to inform Mitre. As a result, the Alliance forces had enough time to prepare themselves and the element of surprise was lost almost immediately.

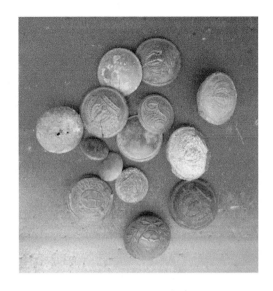

Alliance buttons excavated from the battlefield of Tuyutí. (Courtesy of Vicente Garcia and Vicenta Miranda Ojeda, Museo Paso de Patria and Museo del ex-Cuartel de Mariscal López; author's collection)

The general Paraguayan advance commenced at 11.55 a.m. For simplicity, the description of the battle that follows will explore the fate of each Paraguayan column in turn. The 1st Column, under Barrios, attacked the Brazilians on the left of the Alliance Army; here, the defenders had built a strong redoubt known as Fosso de Mallet, from the name of the Brazilian officer who commanded the artillery. Barrios had some initial success against the enemy infantry, mostly because the latter consisted of only a few units. The Paraguayans almost reached the Alliance tents, but were repulsed by a Brazilian cavalry counterattack that pushed them back to their starting positions.

In the center, the Paraguayans had concentrated two columns and thus hoped to open a large breach in the Alliance front line. Díaz's 3rd Column attacked Flores' Uruguayans, but before it could reach the Alliance artillery, it had to cross a long stretch of marshland. The Paraguayan advance was slowed by the difficult terrain, and thus the Uruguayans were able to use their guns to open up vast holes in the enemy lines. Despite this, the Paraguayans were able to reach the enemy positions and began vicious hand-to-hand fighting with the Uruguayans. The latter were obliged to retreat, and the Brazilians then sent several of their reserve battalions to stop the

The battlefield of Tuyutí as it looks today. (Courtesy of Vicente Garcia and Vicenta Miranda Ojeda, Museo Paso de Patria and Museo del ex-Cuartel de Mariscal López; author's collection)

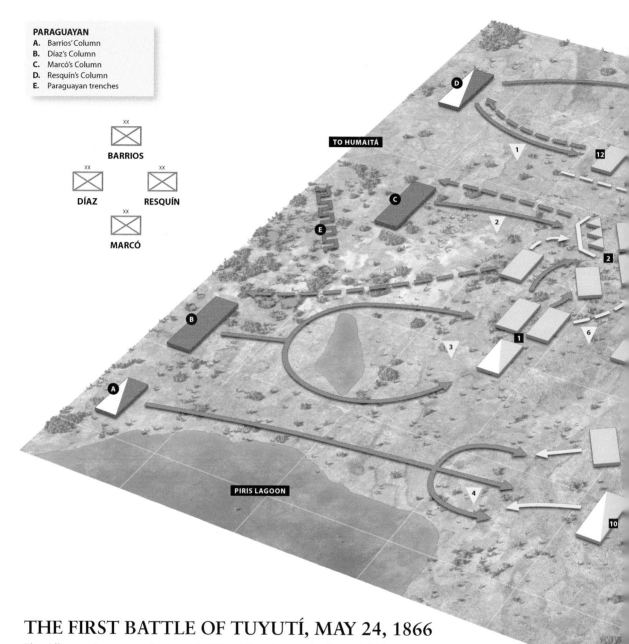

**PARAGUAYAN**
A. Barrios' Column
B. Díaz's Column
C. Marcó's Column
D. Resquín's Column
E. Paraguayan trenches

BARRIOS

DÍAZ          RESQUÍN

MARCÓ

TO HUMAITÁ

PIRIS LAGOON

# THE FIRST BATTLE OF TUYUTÍ, MAY 24, 1866

The Alliance Army, numbering 32,000 soldiers, is attacked by 24,000 Paraguayans just outside its camp at Tuyutí. Despite being pressed hard by the advance of the four Paraguayan attacking columns, the Alliance troops are able to block the enemy assaults and soon launch effective counterattacks.

## EVENTS

**1.** Brigadier-General Resquín's column, comprising two infantry battalions and eight cavalry regiments, attacks the Argentine contingents on the right wing of the Alliance Army.

**2.** Colonel Marcó's column, composed of four infantry battalions and two cavalry regiments, joins Díaz's column in the attack against the center of the Alliance Army.

**3.** Colonel Díaz's column, comprising five infantry battalions and two cavalry regiments, attacks the Uruguayan Division in the center of the Alliance Army.

**4.** General Barrios' column, formed from six infantry battalions and two cavalry regiments, attacks the Brazilian contingents on the left wing of the Alliance Army.

**5.** After some initial success, the hook maneuver of Barrios' column is repulsed by the Brazilian reserves.

**6.** The Uruguayan Division, clearly outnumbered by the Paraguayans, is forced to retreat after suffering heavy losses.

**7.** The sizable Brazilian reserves, mostly Voluntários da Patria units, advance toward the front line in the center of the Alliance Army in order to support the hard-pressed Uruguayans.

**8.** The Argentines, having been partly routed by Resquín's cavalry, are able to launch an effective counterattack with their foot units. The Paraguayans are emphatically repulsed with heavy losses.

Note: gridlines are shown at intervals of 0.62 miles (1km)

N
XXXX
OSÓRIO
XXXX
MITRE
17
16
19
18
8
20
5
22
ARGENTINES
21
BRAZILLIANS
URUGUAYANS
7
9
8
7
11
PARANÀ RIVER
TO PASO DE LA PATRIA
ALLIANCE CAMP
TRIPLE ALLIANCE
Uruguayans and Brazilians
1. Uruguayan Division
2. 10th Brigade (with deployed units)
3. 14th Brigade
4. 12th Brigade
5. 18th Brigade
6. 3rd Division
7. 1st Division
8. 21st Brigade
9. 4th Division
10. Volunteer Cavalry Brigade
11. 5th Cavalry Division
Argentines
12. 2nd Division, I Army Corps
13. 1st Division, I Army Corps
14. 4th Division, I Army Corps
15. 3rd Division, I Army Corps
16. 1st Division, II Army Corps
17. 2nd Division, II Army Corps
18. 3rd Division, II Army Corps
19. 4th Division, II Army Corps
20. Mitre's escort
Headquarters
21. Osório's HQ
22. Mitre's HQ

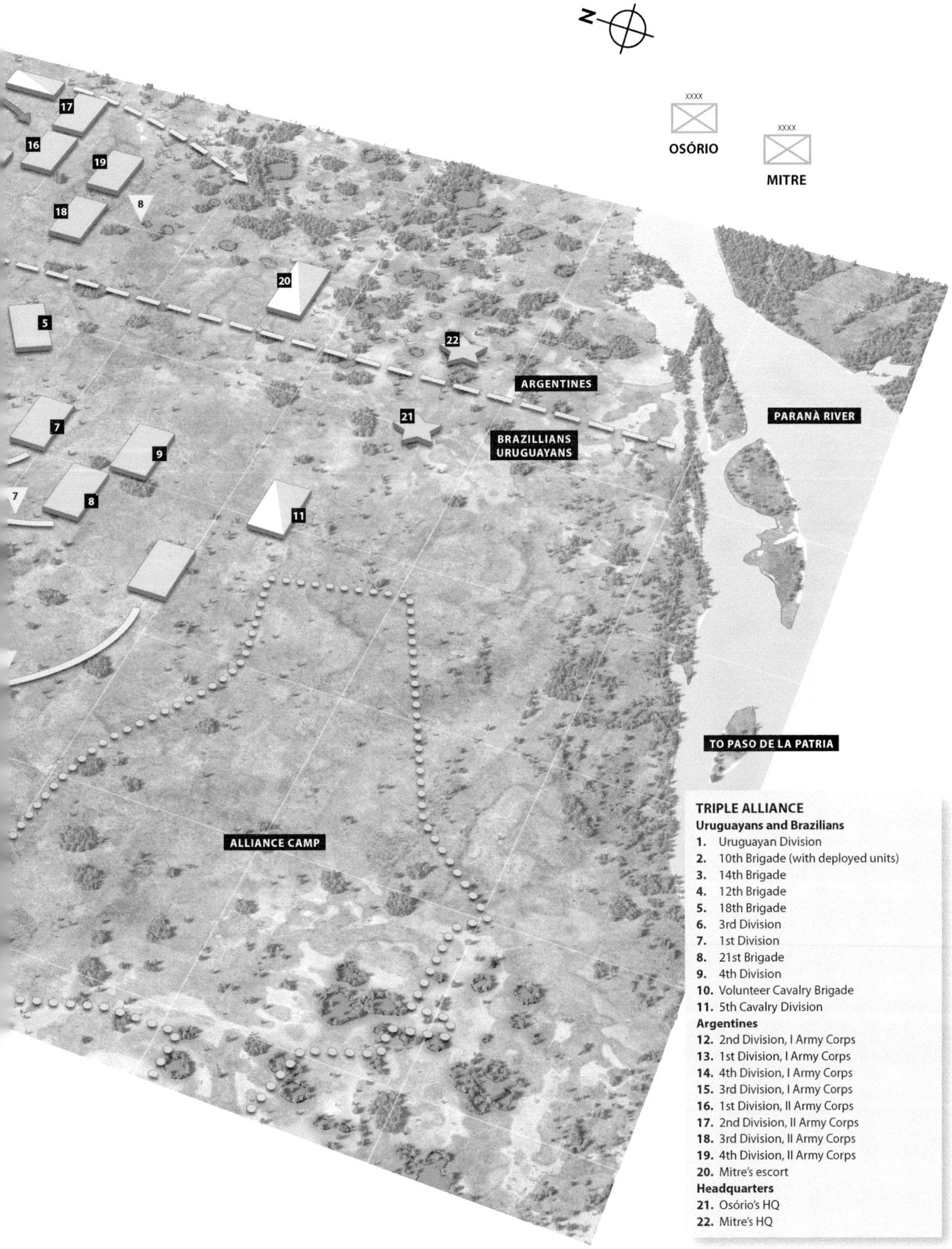

Paraguayan advance. At this point, the Paraguayans turned to assault the Fosso de Mallet on the Alliance left, which was already under attack from Barrios' column. Here, the Brazilians had to put up a desperate resistance in order to keep their positions, and suffered very high casualties. However, the Paraguayans were being destroyed by the Brazilians' Whitworth and La Hitte guns; the shrapnel fire of the defenders pushed back any Paraguayan attempt to overcome the redoubt. As time progressed, the grapeshot of the Alliance guns continued to kill dozens of Paraguayans and their attack began to lose energy. The 4th Column under Marcó, attacking the other redoubt that had been built in the center of the Alliance front line, was more easily repulsed by the defenders.

On the right, the 2nd Column under Resquín soon routed the Argentine mounted units with a cavalry charge, and captured 20 enemy guns; the formidable Paraguayan cavalrymen, however, were too few to face the entire Argentine contingent and lacked infantry support. As a result, the Argentine infantry was able to organize a significant counterattack and almost destroyed the Paraguayan cavalry: the artillery guns lost were recaptured, and the front line in this sector returned to its original position.

During the final phase of the battle, the Paraguayans attempted a desperate double envelopment of the Alliance infantry, using the cavalry from Barrios' column on the left and Resquín's cavalry on the right. The heavy losses suffered by the Paraguayans meant that the plan came to nothing. On the right, Resquín's cavalry was decimated by the infantry battalions of the Argentine reserve, while on the left Barrios' mounted troops were repulsed by a counterattack from the Brazilian volunteer cavalry.

By 4.30 p.m., the Battle of Tuyutí was effectively over: the Alliance had successfully defended its encampment, and the remnants of the Paraguayan forces were retreating back to their original positions. The butcher's bill was heavy: the Paraguayans lost 6,000 soldiers, the Alliance 1,000. López's assault against the Alliance camp had been a disaster: he had lost most of his best men, especially in the cavalry branch. The Alliance had suffered too, but in the end had been able to resist successfully. Both sides learned that their cavalry, although of excellent quality, was no longer able to capture artillery batteries. Rifled guns were the new masters of South America's battlefields.

Argentine line infantrymen attacking the Paraguayans at the Battle of Boquerón del Sauce, on July 18, 1866.

# THE BATTLE OF BOQUERÓN DEL SAUCE, JULY 1866

After the Battle of Tuyutí, the Alliance forces remained in their camp for several months and did not attempt any further advance against the Paraguayans. This was not due to the losses suffered, but to logistical and medical problems: the Alliance Army was short of every kind of supply, and cholera and smallpox were raging through its ranks, causing hundreds of deaths. Moreover, the Paraguayans had not abandoned their positions, and seemed determined to continue the fight. The challenging subtropical climate in these winter months, and the difficult terrain of southern Paraguay, also dissuaded the Alliance from further concerted military activity at this point.

López made good use of this period of Alliance inactivity, building new defensive positions. A large battery was built on the cliffs of Curupaytí, in a strategic site dominating the right flank of the Paraguay River, some five miles downstream from Humaitá. A further, smaller battery was built at Curuzú on the Paraguay River a few miles southwest of Curupaytí. Both these new positions had a dual purpose: they were built to prevent the Brazilian fleet from sailing upriver on the Paraguay to outflank the Paraguayan Army, but were also to be used as fortified positions against a frontal Alliance advance on land. During the long lull in military operations, however, the Paraguayans remained active: they bombarded the Alliance positions frequently and sent small raiding parties against the enemy almost every day. Both these measures, however, had only symbolic value, and achieved little.

Uruguayan soldiers of the Battalion "Florida" at the funeral of their commander Colonel León de Pallejas, who was killed in action at the Battle of Boquerón del Sauce. León de Pallejas was a highly experienced officer, who had previously fought in the First Carlist War (1833–40), the Uruguayan Civil War (1839–51) and the Platine War (1851–52).

A Uruguayan field battery in action at the Battle of Boquerón del Sauce.

López did his best to replenish his reduced army with new recruits, and after a few months, he was able to bring the total number of soldiers under his command to 20,000. Skirmishing between the two armies continued for several weeks, occasionally reaching the status of "small battle." Among these was the July 11, 1866 Battle of Yataytí Corá, in which the Paraguayans launched a two-column raid against the Argentine positions. This encounter cost the Paraguayans 400 dead.

During the night of July 13/14, López ordered the construction of three trenches close to the Brazilian left flank. He planned for Paraguayan snipers and artillery to use these to attack the enemy troops and camp. The Paraguayans managed to maintain absolute silence while they worked for most of the night, and by the beginning of the next day, when they were discovered by Alliance sentries, the three trenches were almost complete. The Brazilians responded with intense artillery fire, but this had little effect.

On July 16, 3,000 Alliance soldiers were sent to storm the newly built Paraguayan trenches. They were able to rapidly occupy the first trench, but then came under heavy fire from the Paraguayan defenders who had abandoned it. The battle continued for 16 hours, during which the Paraguayans launched several counterattacks to regain their previous positions. Having lost 2,000 men, López decided enough was enough, and ordered a retreat. The Paraguayans, who had come close to victory at Tuyutí, had once again showed their courage and determination.

On July 18, the Alliance launched a further assault, this time on the two remaining trenches, that was initially repulsed with heavy losses. Attacks and counterattacks followed for several hours, during which an increasing number of Alliance soldiers were transferred to the left wing of the camp.

The sinking of the Brazilian ironclad *Río de Janeiro*. On September 1, 1866, this warship bombarded the Paraguayan fortifications at Curuzú alongside the other Brazilian ironclads. On the next day, a 68 lb shell entered one of her gunports during the bombardment, killing four men and wounding five. After the damage had been repaired, the ship struck two mines and sank.

Seeing this, López launched an attack against the Argentine contingent on the right with cavalry supported by rocket-launchers. The clash was on the verge of turning into a large pitched battle, but in the end the Paraguayan cavalry attack was repulsed and López's new trenches were finally occupied by the Alliance. Collectively, the two clashes became known as the Battle of Boquerón del Sauce; they resulted in no gain for the Paraguayans, but cost the Alliance a large number of skilled soldiers and officers.

# THE BATTLES OF CURUZÚ AND CURUPAYTÍ, SEPTEMBER 1866

The Alliance decided once again to resume the advance against key Paraguayan positions. Their principle target was the Paraguayan battery of Curupaytí; the latter presented a formidable obstacle to any further movements of the Alliance fleet on the Paraguay River. It was decided that the battery would be bombarded by the Brazilian warships. In the meantime, the battery at Curupaytí had been reinforced with the addition of other guns (bringing the total to 25, later 38) and with a newly built defensive line, which encompassed the wider area around the battery.

In order to bombard Curupaytí, the Alliance ships first had to destroy the southern battery at Curuzú. On September 1, 1866, five Brazilian ironclads were dispatched to do this, but to little effect. The following day, the Brazilians attacked again, but this time the Paraguayan response was highly effective, and caused heavy damage to the ironclad *Río de Janeiro*. Meanwhile, the Alliance landed 8,000 men near Las Palmas, on the eastern bank of the Paraguay River, with the objective of attacking Curuzú by land. The Brazilians, however, were unaware of the new Paraguayan defensive line built around Curupaytí, which began at Curuzú; the line made their approach to the battery very difficult. The Brazilians were finally able to reach the Paraguayan positions from the rear, and the ensuing September 3 land attack, conducted by two columns with a simultaneous naval bombardment, was a complete success. A large number of the Paraguayan defenders, however, retreated back to Curupaytí, escaping capture. For the first time in the war, the Brazilian fleet had revealed its deficiencies when attacking land batteries.

After the fall of Curuzú, the Paraguayans reinforced their defensive positions at Curupaytí by sending more guns and troops to garrison the battery. López intended to stop the Alliance advance with a defensive battle, seeking to inflict the largest possible number of casualties on the enemy.

The defenses of Curupaytí were formidable. They were located in a narrow area between the Paraguay River to the east and Lake López to the west; the latter comprised only shallow water, but covered most of the Paraguayan battery in the center and on the right and thus formed a significant obstacle for the advancing Alliance troops. The Paraguayans began work on reinforcing their defenses on September 8, 1866, under the direction of three foreign engineer officers, employed by López for their technical expertise: Colonel Francisco Wisner de Morgenstern, Lieutenant-Colonel George Thompson, and Lieutenant-Colonel Leopoldo Myzkonski. The Paraguayan garrison worked day and night, with great determination: the Alliance forces were very near and thus the new defenses had to be constructed under conditions of total silence. All the trees in the area to the fore of the battery

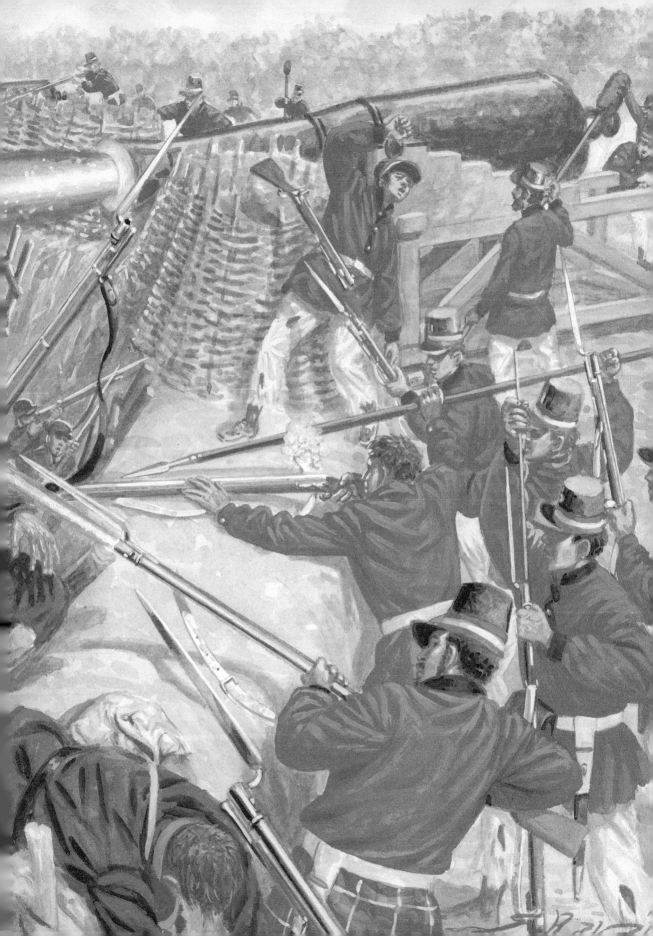

## THE BATTLE OF CURUPAYTÍ, SEPTEMBER 22, 1866 (PP. 68–69)

The Alliance attack started in the early morning of September 22, with the Brazilian fleet under Admiral Tamandaré bombarding the Paraguayan positions with eight warships and three gunboats. Then, at noon, the four land columns started their advance against the first line of enemy trenches. The advancing infantrymen were soon cut down by fire from the Paraguayan guns. Only some of the Argentine infantry, on the center-right, were briefly able to reach the top of the enemy earthen rampart, before being repulsed by the Paraguayan infantry. This particular moment is reproduced

here in the illustration. The Argentine infantrymen (**1**), all from the *cazadores* (light) companies of their respective battalions, are dressed in dark blue with distinctive green facings. Their officers (**2**) wear French-style uniforms, with Hungarian knots on the sleeves and loose trousers. The Paraguayans (**3**), despite being equipped with flintlock muskets and not percussion ones like the Argentines, could count on the numerous heavy guns placed in their defensive positions (**4**).

were felled, and the wood used to erect a palisade in another defensive line further south. The Paraguayan defensive system thus comprised the following elements, in order: a forward ditch and wooden palisade; a killing zone of broken, treeless terrain; and the trenches proper of Curupaytí, mounting a large number of heavy guns, on cliffs that dominated both the Paraguay River and the killing zone. This second line of trenches was protected by an earth wall (2.75m wide and 2.1m high) and by a deep defensive ditch. The works were completed in a few days and the Alliance had no idea of their existence: López's plan, at least on this occasion, was working well.

Bartolomé Mitre (left) and Francisco Solano López (right) at the Yataytí Corá peace talks, on September 12, 1866. López hoped to convince the Argentine president to abandon the Triple Alliance and offered him the possibility of a separate peace.

In order to gain time and in hopes of finding a compromise with Argentina, on September 12, Francisco Solano López met with Mitre and Flores at Yataytí Corá. The Alliance leaders, who both wanted to end the war as soon as possible in order to deal with their respective internal problems, proposed a temporary exile in Europe for the Paraguayan dictator. The latter refused, but his participation in the meeting had given his soldiers extra time to complete their preparations.

After the failure of the peace talks, the Alliance leadership decided on a frontal land attack on the Paraguayan positions at Curupaytí: it would be led by the Argentines, since the Brazilians were still recovering from the losses incurred during the previous battles. The Argentines would be supported by an intense naval bombardment from the Brazilian fleet, which was to attack the Paraguayan battery from the river. The Alliance leadership, however, had little idea of what awaited them: a total of 49 guns, 12 of them heavy 68-pdrs. Most of these were deployed aiming toward the south, since only 13 guns (including four heavy 68-pdrs) faced the river. The positions of the river and the lake made flank attacks impossible; in addition, the 13 guns facing the river would make any attempt to disembark troops to the rear of Curupaytí very difficult. A frontal attack was the only possible option, even though this would cause heavy Alliance casualties. However, the Alliance was confident that the Brazilian naval bombardment fleet would destroy most of the Paraguayan defenses.

A contemporary painting showing the Paraguayan defensive line at the Battle of Curupaytí, September 22, 1866. Heavy artillery pieces were evenly distributed along the Paraguayan line in strong redoubts, while ammunition and weapons were stored in small bunkers made of wood and earth (note the domed structures in the foreground). The heavy cannon at the center of the scene is almost certainly a 68-pdr.

The Alliance attacking force was organized into four columns: the two smaller ones, made up of Brazilians, would attack the eastern sector near the river, while the two larger ones, made up of Argentines, would assault the center and western sector after crossing the lake. The Paraguayan defenders numbered just 5,000, consisting of seven infantry battalions and four dismounted cavalry regiments; the Alliance forces were around 18,000 strong.

# ORDERS OF BATTLE, CURUPAYTÍ, SEPTEMBER 22, 1866

## PARAGUAYAN

Overall commander: General José Díaz

### CAVALRY (LEFT FLANK)

Commander: Captain Bernardino Caballero
6th Cavalry Regiment
8th Cavalry Regiment
9th Cavalry Regiment
36th Cavalry Regiment

### INFANTRY (CENTER AND RIGHT FLANK)

Commander: Colonel Antonio Luis González
4th Infantry Battalion
7th Infantry Battalion
9th Infantry Battalion
27th Infantry Battalion
36th Infantry Battalion
38th Infantry Battalion
40th Infantry Battalion

## ALLIANCE

### 1ST COLUMN; BRAZILIANS (LEFT FLANK)

Commander: Colonel Augusto Caldas
**2nd Infantry Brigade**
11th Infantry Battalion
5th Corpo de Voluntários da Pátria Battalion
8th Corpo de Voluntários da Pátria Battalion
12th Corpo de Voluntários da Pátria Battalion
**3rd Infantry Brigade**
18th Corpo de Voluntários da Pátria Battalion
32nd Corpo de Voluntários da Pátria Battalion
26th Corpo de Voluntários da Pátria Battalion
**7th Cavalry Brigade**
VII National Guard Cavalry Corps
VIII National Guard Cavalry Corps
IX National Guard Cavalry Corps

### 2ND COLUMN; BRAZILIANS (LEFT FLANK)

Commander: General Albino de Carvalho
**Auxiliary Brigade**
6th Infantry Battalion
10th Corpo de Voluntários da Pátria Battalion
11th Corpo de Voluntários da Pátria Battalion
20th Corpo de Voluntários da Pátria Battalion
46th Corpo de Voluntários da Pátria Battalion
**1st Infantry Brigade**
29th Corpo de Voluntários da Pátria Battalion
34th Corpo de Voluntários da Pátria Battalion

47th Corpo de Voluntários da Pátria Battalion
**4th Cavalry Brigade**
I Corps of Mounted Rifles
II Corps of Mounted Rifles
V Corps of Mounted Rifles

### 3RD COLUMN; ARGENTINES (CENTER)

Commander: General Wenceslao Paunero
**1st Infantry Division**
1st Infantry Battalion
5th Infantry Battalion
Legión Militár Infantry Battalion
National Guard Infantry Battalion San Nicolás
**2nd Infantry Division**
4th Infantry Battalion
6th Infantry Battalion
2nd Infantry Battalion
1st Legion of Volunteers
**3rd Infantry Division**
National Guard Infantry Battalion Corrientes
National Guard Infantry Battalion Rosario
National Guard Infantry Battalion Catamarca
National Guard Infantry Battalion Tucumán
**4th Infantry Division**
3rd Infantry Battalion
2nd Legion of Volunteers
National Guard Infantry Battalion Santa Fé
National Guard Infantry Battalion Salta

### 4TH COLUMN; ARGENTINES (RIGHT FLANK)

Commander: General Bartolomé Mitre
**1st Infantry Division**
1st National Guard Infantry Battalion of Buenos Aires
2nd National Guard Infantry Battalion of Buenos Aires
3rd National Guard Infantry Battalion of Buenos Aires
4th National Guard Infantry Battalion of Buenos Aires
**2nd Infantry Division**
5th National Guard Infantry Battalion of Buenos Aires
6th National Guard Infantry Battalion of Buenos Aires
7th National Guard Infantry Battalion of Buenos Aires
8th National Guard Infantry Battalion of Buenos Aires
**3rd Infantry Division**
National Guard Infantry Battalion Córdoba
National Guard Infantry Battalion San Juán
National Guard Infantry Battalion Segundo de Entre Ríos
National Guard Infantry Battalion Mendoza
**4th Infantry Division**
9th Infantry Battalion
12th Infantry Battalion
National Guard Infantry Battalion Tercero de Entre Ríos
National Guard Infantry Battalion La Rioja

The Alliance attack started early on the morning of September 22. The Brazilian fleet, under the command of Admiral Joaquim Marques Lisboa, Marquis of Tamandaré, bombarded the Paraguayan positions with eight warships and three gunboats. The naval bombardment lasted for five hours, but caused little damage and few casualties.

As soon as the warships ceased firing, at noon, the four land columns began their advance against the first line of Paraguayan trenches, unaware that a further line had been built to the south. The advancing infantrymen carried fascines to fill the ditch and rudimentary ladders to scale the earth bank. The Alliance attack began well, with the first line of enemy trenches soon passed and little resistance encountered. The Paraguayans had been ordered to retreat to the battery as soon as the Alliance troops approached the first defensive line. The killing zone between the two trenches was mostly under water, due to recent rainfall: the retreating Paraguayans, who knew the area intimately, were able to cross it with ease, whereas the Alliance troops were slowed by the terrain and presented an easy target for the Paraguayan artillery.

The trenches of Curupaytí as they look today. (Courtesy of Vicente Garcia and Vicenta Miranda Ojeda, Museo Paso de Patria and Museo del ex-Cuartel de Mariscal López; author's collection)

The field pieces supporting the Alliance advance were slow to arrive, and the Alliance soldiers soon learnt that the Brazilian naval bombardment had achieved almost nothing. The Paraguayan guns opened up with a terrible fire of grape, canister, and shell: in the space of a few minutes, hundreds of Brazilian and Argentine infantrymen had been felled, killed, or wounded. The Alliance soldiers continued their advance with great courage, but most of them were slain before they could reach the Paraguayan second trench line. Only some of the Argentine infantry companies, in the center-right, were briefly able to reach the top of the enemy earthen bank. They were soon repulsed, however, by the Paraguayan infantry, who opened up a deadly fire with their muskets and engaged the assaulting troops with their bayonets.

The interior of the Paraguayan trenches at Curupaytí. (Courtesy of Vicente Garcia and Vicenta Miranda Ojeda, Museo Paso de Patria and Museo del ex-Cuartel de Mariscal López; author's collection)

By 5 p.m., the Alliance attack had come to an end, and the killing zone was littered with the dead, dying, and wounded. Mitre ordered a general retreat, while the Paraguayans dispatched one of their infantry battalions south of the cliffs, in order to kill all the wounded enemy soldiers who remained on the field, and to strip the corpses of any weapons or items of equipment that could be reused. The Alliance losses had been terrible: 2,200 Argentines and 2,000 Brazilians; the Paraguayans, in contrast, suffered only 100 casualties.

The Battle of Curupaytí was a turning point in the war: it was the greatest defeat suffered by the Alliance up to that point, and encouraged Paraguay to continue the struggle. López had shown his enemies and his people that he was able to defend Paraguayan national territory from foreign invasion, while the Alliance had learnt that conquering Paraguay would be extremely difficult and costly in terms of lives. With such a strong defensive position still intact, the Paraguayans could now safely reorganize their military forces, while the Alliance troops were forced to return to their original camp at Tuyutí to recover from the losses suffered.

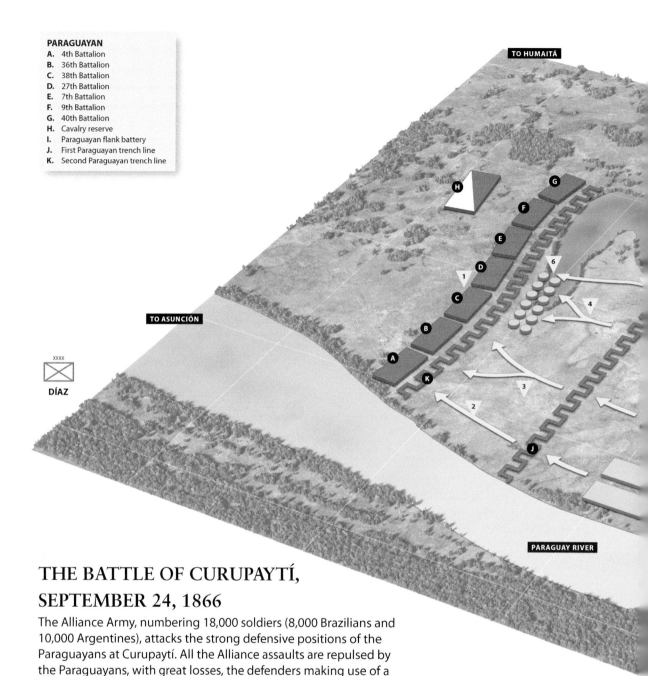

**PARAGUAYAN**

- **A.** 4th Battalion
- **B.** 36th Battalion
- **C.** 38th Battalion
- **D.** 27th Battalion
- **E.** 7th Battalion
- **F.** 9th Battalion
- **G.** 40th Battalion
- **H.** Cavalry reserve
- **I.** Paraguayan flank battery
- **J.** First Paraguayan trench line
- **K.** Second Paraguayan trench line

TO HUMAITÁ

TO ASUNCIÓN

DÍAZ

PARAGUAY RIVER

# THE BATTLE OF CURUPAYTÍ, SEPTEMBER 24, 1866

The Alliance Army, numbering 18,000 soldiers (8,000 Brazilians and 10,000 Argentines), attacks the strong defensive positions of the Paraguayans at Curupaytí. All the Alliance assaults are repulsed by the Paraguayans, with great losses, the defenders making use of a large number of heavy artillery pieces and two lines of trenches.

## EVENTS

**1.** The preparatory fire from the Brazilian fleet has little effect on the Paraguayan defenses at Curupaytí, and they remain largely intact. In total, the Paraguayan soldiers number only 5,000, but can count on 50 artillery pieces.

**2.** There are four Alliance attacking columns: two are made up of Brazilian troops and two of Argentine soldiers. The advance of the Brazilian 1st Column, having overrun the first line of Paraguayan trenches, is stopped.

**3.** The Brazilian 2nd Column, after a long advance under fire, is forced to the left and attacks the same sector of the Paraguayan trenches that has been assaulted by the Brazilian 1st Column.

**4.** The Argentine 3rd Column approaches its objective: two of the divisions that make up the column detach all their light infantry companies in order to form

a special assault force. These soldiers are able to break through the first line of Paraguayan trenches and begin to assault the second one.

**5.** The Argentine 4th Column advances with just two brigades, to attack a secondary sector of the Paraguayan defenses.

**6.** The Argentines detach the *cazadores* to attack the Paraguayan second trench line with a bayonet assault, but they are repulsed by the Paraguayan infantry, with crippling losses.

**7.** The Argentine 4th Column is able to overrun the first Paraguayan trench line and joins the main Argentine assault against the Paraguayan center.

**8.** In a secondary sector of the battle, the Paraguayans deploy a field battery to harass the Argentine flank. The Argentines respond by engaging their artillery reserve, which initiates an artillery duel with the Paraguayan battery.

Note: gridlines are shown at intervals of 0.62 miles (1km)

**TRIPLE ALLIANCE**
**Brazilian:**
1. 3rd Brigade (1st Column)
2. 2nd Brigade (1st Column)
3. 7th Cavalry Brigade (1st Column)
4. 1st Brigade (2nd Column)
5. Auxiliary Brigade (2nd Column)
6. 4th Cavalry Brigade (2nd Column)
**Argentine:**
7. 4th Division, I Army Corps (3rd Column)
8. 1st Division, I Army Corps (3rd Column)
9. 2nd Division, I Army Corps (3rd Column)
10. 3rd Division, I Army Corps (3rd Column)
11. 4th Division, II Army Corps (4th Column)
12. 3rd Division, II Army Corps (4th Column)
13. 2nd Division, II Army Corps (4th Column)
14. 1st Division, II Army Corps (4th Column)
**Camp:**
15. Brazilian camp

ARGENTINES

BRAZILIANS

XXXX
MITRE

TO PASO DE PATRIA

# THE LONG STALEMATE, SEPTEMBER 1866– JULY 1867

After Curupaytí, the Alliance Army remained inactive for ten whole months, until July 1867. During this long lull in military operations, the Alliance continued to lose thousands of men and animals through sickness and a lack of food. The complete lack of hygiene and the logistical difficulties made the large encampment of Tuyutí a deadly place: without food and medicine, survival became a challenge, especially in remote, foreign territory that had been devastated by months of war. All these difficulties greatly impacted the morale of the Alliance soldiers, who started to desert en masse. Discipline and organization soon broke down, notably in the first months following the disaster at Curupaytí.

Moreover, serious differences in opinion began to arise betwee the Triple Alliance members: the Argentines and the Uruguayans were tired of war and were ready to negotiate with the enemy, but the Brazilians wanted to continue until the Paraguayan dictator was dead. The Uruguayan contingent was by now reduced to a few hundred soldiers, while the Argentines decided to send home the majority of their military units. The Brazilians also experienced manpower problems: the flow of enthusiastic volunteers who wished to enter the *Corpo de Voluntários da Pátria* battalions fell steadily after Curupaytí.

The Paraguayans, having learned from their success at Curupaytí, attempted to improve their land defenses by connecting the Curupaytí battery to the Fortress of Humaitá with a system of trenches. Every able-bodied man in the country, including boys and slaves, was forced to serve in the Paraguayan Army in order to augment the total number of available soldiers.

During the long pause in military operations, the British, French, and American governments tried to mediate between the opposing sides in order to bring the war to an end. Despite their best efforts, however, all the diplomatic maneuvering came to nothing.

Stirrups excavated from the battlefield of Tuyutí. (Courtesy of Vicente Garcia and Vicenta Miranda Ojeda, Museo Paso de Patria and Museo del ex-Cuartel de Mariscal López; author's collection)

Mitre, commander-in-chief of the Alliance Army, had to abandon the front on two separate occasions in order to face down Federalist agitation and Amerindian violence that erupted in Argentina. Flores had to deal with the *Blancos* opposition to the war; having returned to Uruguay, he never again returned to Paraguay (on February 19, 1868, he was assassinated in Montevideo).

On November 18, 1866, the Duke of Caxias was nominated overall commander of the Brazilian Army, and was tasked with restoring discipline and order in the ranks of the Imperial military. Caxias had already demonstrated his capability on numerous occasions during his long career, most notably fighting the gaucho rebels in the *Farrapos* Revolt, and thus was the perfect man to help the Alliance out of its crisis. Restoring morale was a key factor in this process, together with a general improvement in logistics. Caxias requested the dispatch of hundreds of new weapons to the front and ordered the creation of a new Balloon Corps for observing enemy positions; the deficiencies in reconnaissance had been among the most important causes of the Curupaytí defeat.

The Alliance invasion of Paraguay, 1866–67

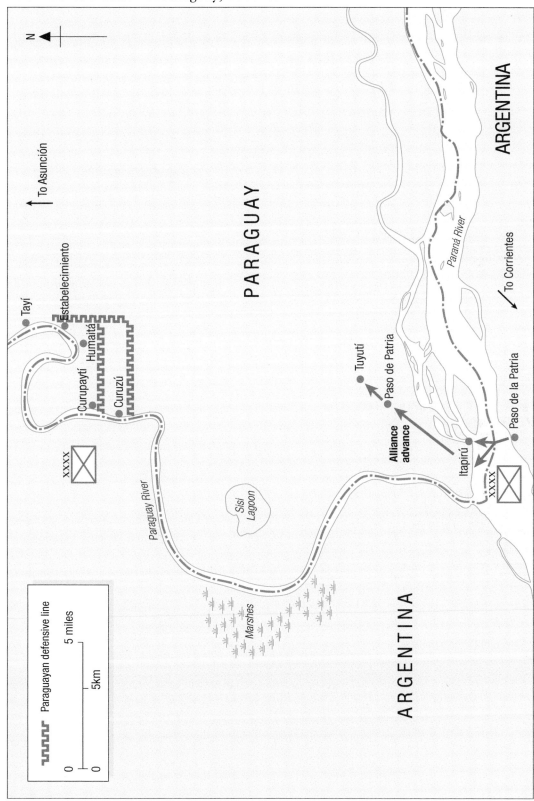

A Brazilian belt buckle found at the battlefield of Tuyutí. (Courtesy of Vicente Garcia and Vicenta Miranda Ojeda, Museo Paso de Patria and Museo del ex-Cuartel de Mariscal López; author's collection)

In addition, Caxias completely reorganized most of the Brazilian Army's units: many *Corpo de Voluntários da Pátria* units were disbanded or merged together, while the regular infantry was expanded with the formation of several new battalions. When Mitre returned to Argentina for the second time, Caxias became the new commander-in-chief of the Alliance Army, effective October 10, 1866.

On August 15, 1867, the Alliance resumed offensive operations and sent two divisions of the Brazilian fleet upriver on the Paraguay. These had to pass both Curupaytí and Humaitá, in order to block the constant flow of supplies coming into the Paraguayan river positions. Paraguayan fire from Curupaytí caused serious damage to the Brazilian warships, but both divisions were able to pass the battery. At this point, one of the two divisions remained in the section of river between Curupaytí and Humaitá, while the other continued north. As they neared the Paraguayan fortress, however, the Brazilian ships decided to halt, in order to better organize their passage in front of Humaitá. Meanwhile, the Alliance had built a road on the Chaco side of the Paraguay River, in order to supply their naval divisions by land.

Caxias' plan was by now clear: he wished to besiege Humaitá as soon as possible, and wanted to capture the fortress by siege and not by launching futile frontal attacks. By blocking the Paraguay River north of Humaitá, the large fortress garrison would soon run out of food and other supplies. Then, with the fall of Humaitá to the north, the southern defensive position of Curupaytí would be in no condition to resist. Caxias' plan to use the Chaco side of the Paraguay River for moving north, instead of advancing frontally north of Tuyutí, was a clever one. The Paraguayans did not expect such a move, because the Chaco comprised a desert region with few natural resources and where the construction of a usable road was considered impossible. The Brazilians, however, were able to move troops and materials across the Chaco, and surprised the Paraguayans. On November 2, 1867, a Brazilian force of 5,000 soldiers was sent north across the Chaco and then crossed the Paraguay to capture the small village of Tayí (north of Humaitá). The small Paraguayan garrison there was taken by surprise. The Brazilians soon reinforced their newly won positions at Tayí by bringing in artillery and by building trenches: the Paraguayans were gradually being encircled by the Alliance forces, who were now ready to begin the blockade of Humaitá.

## THE SECOND BATTLE OF TUYUTÍ, AND THE FALL OF HUMAITÁ

Francisco Solano López rapidly realized that the situation was changing, as the Duke of Caxias had begun to outflank his positions on both his left and right. Both Curupaytí and Humaitá were in grave danger of becoming isolated, and thus the whole Paraguayan defensive system could fall. In a final attempt to break the Alliance's morale, the Paraguayan dictator planned a new attack against the main enemy camp at Tuyutí.

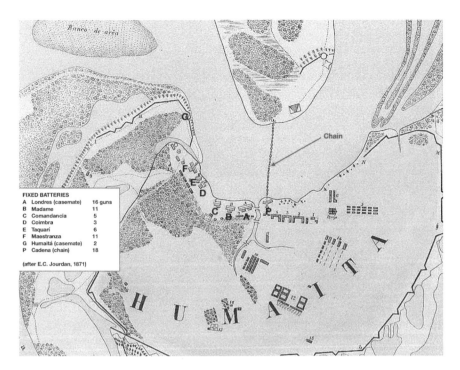

FIXED BATTERIES

| | | |
|---|---|---|
| A | Londres (casemate) | 16 guns |
| B | Madame | 11 |
| C | Comandancia | 5 |
| D | Coimbra | 3 |
| E | Taquari | 6 |
| F | Maestranza | 11 |
| G | Humaitá (casemate) | 2 |
| P | Cadena (chain) | 18 |

(after E.C. Jourdan, 1871)

A Brazilian map (created by E. C. Jourdan) of Humaitá, known as the "Paraguayan Sebastopol." López's main fortress had an extensive complex of brick-built bastions and casemates mounting 62 artillery pieces of different calibers, distributed in eight batteries. These were built on a superb defensive site commanding a sharp S-bend in the Paraguay River (10m above the level of the river). Most of these dominated the narrows, which were protected by a massive chain-boom and two rows of explosive mines.

The general plan was little different to that of the First Battle of Tuyutí: a surprise attack conducted at dawn, while the Alliance soldiers were still sleeping. The Paraguayan infantry would advance on the camp from the east, with 16 battalions, in order to fix the front of the battle; the six regiments of Paraguayan cavalry would outflank the Alliance camp in order to sweep through the tents and capture as much materiel as possible. In total, the Paraguayan soldiers involved numbered only 9,000, but it is important to note that there were fewer Alliance troops in the encampment than during the previous battle.

On November 2, 1867, the Paraguayan infantry, organized into three columns, attacked. Initially, they overcame the first line of Alliance defenses with few losses. The Paraguayans entered the camp and burned to the ground all the structures they found; at this point, with the sun beginning to rise in the sky, the attackers discovered that the Alliance forces had built a new artillery redoubt in the center of the camp. Its guns soon opened fire, causing numerous deaths among the Paraguayans. With little energy left to assault the redoubt, the Paraguayans began a long retreat that was disrupted by a fierce counterattack from the Brazilian infantry. Meanwhile, the Paraguayan cavalry had completed its outflanking maneuver to the east and was now charging the rear of the Alliance camp. However, they soon learnt that their infantry was retreating and they would not be able to join up with the Paraguayan foot. The Argentine cavalry launched a counterattack and forced the Paraguayan cavalry to retreat too, ending the battle. Paraguayan losses amounted to 2,000 men, while Alliance casualties were few.

Caxias now held the initiative. Brazilian preparations for the naval bombardment of Humaitá included the building of three new monitors, which mounted heavy artillery guns specifically designed to heavily damage the Paraguayan fortress. These arrived in theater during the closing weeks of 1867. Meanwhile, López, fearing the collapse of his defenses, had ordered

the construction of a new redoubt north of Humaitá, at Establecimiento: this was completed on February 14, 1868 and was manned by 500 soldiers with nine guns. Since the new redoubt menaced their positions at Tayí, the Alliance forces attacked Establecimiento a few days after the Paraguayan works had been completed. This time, the defenders were too few in number to resist, and, having fired their last rounds of ammunition, were forced to surrender.

By the end of February 1868, the Paraguay River had become deep enough to permit the safe passage of Brazilian warships: during the warmer months, Alliance ships risked grounding on hidden sandbanks or striking the numerous mines and torpedoes that the Paraguayans had anchored in the river.

Humaitá deserved its sobriquet of the "Paraguayan Sebastopol": it featured an extensive complex of brick-built bastions and casemates mounting 62 artillery pieces of different caliber, distributed across eight batteries. These were built on a superb defensive site commanding a sharp S-bend in the Paraguay River, 10m above the level of the river; most of them dominated narrow channels, which were protected by a massive chain-boom and two lines of explosive mines. In the bend, known as the Vuelta de Humaitá, the navigable channel narrowed to just 200m in width and was characterized by strong currents. The eight batteries, each bearing a distinctive name, were laid out in the following order: Humaitá—two guns in a casemate; Maestranza—11 guns; Taquarí—six guns; Coimbra—three guns; Comandancia—five guns; Madame Lynch—11 guns; Londres—16 guns in a casemate; Cadena—18 guns, protecting the chain-boom. The latter was formed from seven different chains, which below the waterline were bound together into three chains. Moreover, communications with Humaitá were excellent, because it was connected to the electrical telegraph lines installed on López's orders. In the course of the war, the number of guns in the batteries was increased to 93, some of which had been captured from the Alliance.

On February 19, 1868, the Brazilian fleet, including the three new monitors, advanced toward the Paraguayan fortress. Since the chain-boom at

A period photo of the port at the Fortress of Humaitá, after its capture by the Alliance in July 1868. Humaitá soon became a very important logistical base for the Brazilian Navy, especially during the final operations of the war.

Humaitá was secured on two barges in order to keep it above the water level, the first objective of the Brazilians was to sink these. This was easily achieved by the Brazilian warships, having passed by the Paraguayan batteries without suffering major damage. Despite the negative prediction, the fire from the Paraguayan heavy artillery was unable to penetrate the thick plate armor of the Brazilian ironclads, and thus, after an hour's fighting, the fleet passed Humaitá and reached the Alliance positions at Tayí. Some Brazilian warships would require several weeks' worth of repairs before returning to action, but for this cost the Alliance had achieved a great victory: Humaitá and its large garrison were now cut off. In addition, the Brazilian naval squadron was not at liberty to sail further upriver and bombard the Paraguayan capital of Asunción, which was carried out for the first time on February 24. The day before this, however, the Paraguayans had evacuated the city and transferred their government to the village of Luque. After this symbolic act, which caused little material damage, the Brazilian ships returned to Tayí.

Knowing full well that Humaitá would fall if the Brazilian naval blockade was not broken, López ordered an attack by infantry in canoes against the Brazilian warships in an effort to board at least one of them. This assault, launched on March 2, came close to succeeding, with two Brazilian ships temporarily boarded by the Paraguayans. The arrival of the rest of the Brazilian fleet, however, eventually resulted in the death of all members of this raiding force. It had been a desperate attempt, but the Paraguayans had few other options since the remnants of their fleet were in no condition to fight the Brazilian ironclads.

López now decided that the time had come to withdraw his forces from the defenses around Curupaytí and Humaitá. All the artillery pieces emplaced in the various trenches and defensive positions were taken to Humaitá, leaving just six guns in the battery at Curupaytí; from the fortress, these guns were transferred further north, using the last two steamers of the Paraguayan Navy still in service. Once the whole operation was completed, just a few thousand Paraguayan soldiers remained to face the Alliance forces, with almost no guns. Since the garrison of Humaitá was also mostly evacuated, the 1,500 Alliance prisoners in the fortress were all executed by the Paraguayans.

Between March 21 and 23, 1868, the Alliance launched a general offensive against the Paraguayan defenses south of Humaitá. These were soon overcome, including the battery at Curupaytí, without great difficulty; most of the trenches had been abandoned by the few defenders before the enemy assault. At the same time, the last two Paraguayan warships were eliminated by the Brazilian fleet. In the following weeks, the Alliance bombarded Humaitá using their fleet almost daily. When the land artillery joined the bombardment from the south, it became clear that all hope was lost for the defenders, and capture or death were their only prospects. The Paraguayans rapidly ran out of food and ammunition, and were unable to respond to the Alliance guns.

On July 24, the Paraguayans attempted to evacuate their forces from Humaitá. Initially, they managed to avoid detection by the Alliance forces, but soon the Brazilian ships intervened to impede the Paraguayans from crossing the river, and most of the retreating Paraguayans were captured. When the Alliance troops entered the fortress, they found it completely deserted. After weeks of blockade and bombardment, the greatest fortress in South America had fallen.

## THE PIKYSYRY MANEUVER, AND THE BEGINNING OF THE *DEZEMBRADA*, 1868

The Paraguayans retreated north, halting just south of their capital Asunción to organize a new defensive line. López was determined to continue war to the bitter end, despite the fact that his military resources were dwindling. The new Paraguayan defensive line, built rapidly and with the few available raw materials, began at two formidable river batteries at Angostura on the banks of the Paraguay River, and stretched along the Pikysyry Stream.

López's principle objective was to protect his capital. Most of the population were by now extremely weary of the war and some were ready to rise in revolt. A frontal attack on the new Paraguayan defensive system would cost the Alliance both time and lives, which Caxias was keen to avoid. The Angostura batteries (one with eight guns, and one with seven) prevented the Brazilian fleet from outflanking the defenses to the west, while to the east of the Pikysyry Line lay marshland that could not be crossed by a large army.

The Alliance commander-in-chief was thus forced to come up with an alternative plan, which later became known as the Pikysyry Maneuver. He planned to ship a large portion of the Alliance Army to the west bank of the Paraguay River. A small contingent from this force would then build a wooden corduroy road stretching several miles through the Chaco marshes, which would then be used by the remaining units to move north. After bypassing the

An engraving (dated January 29, 1870) showing the Paraguayan encampment and López's headquarters, located six miles from Angostura on the hill of Pikysyry.

# The Alliance campaign of 1868–69 in Paraguay

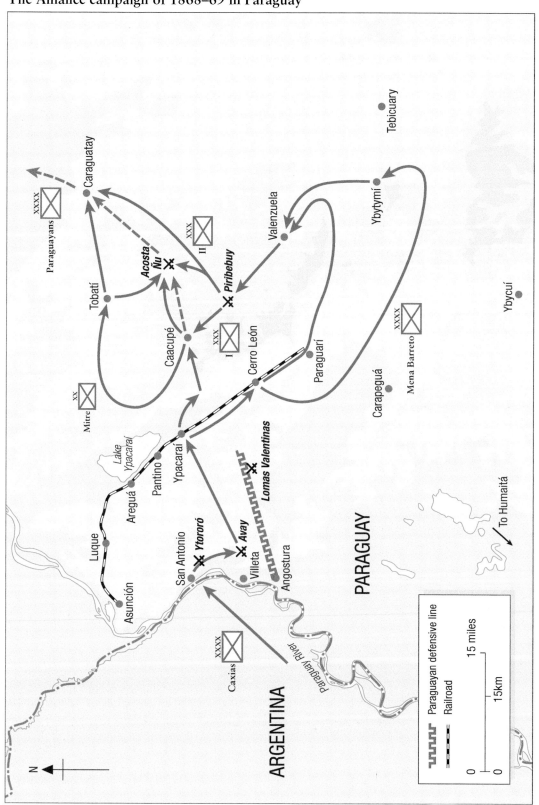

Tebicuary

Caraguatay

XXXX Paraguayans

Valenzuela

XXX II

*Acosta Ñu*

Tobatí

*Piribebuy*

Ybytymí

Caacupé

XXX I Cerro León

XX Mitre

Ybycuí

Paraguarí

Mena Barreto XXXX

Lake Ypacaraí

Carapeguá

Pantino

Ypacaraí

Areguá

*Lomas Valentinas*

Luque

*Ytororó*

*Avay*

San Antonio

Asunción

Villeta

Angostura

To Humaitá

PARAGUAY

Caxias XXXX

Paraguay River

ARGENTINA

N

Paraguayan defensive line

Railroad

15 miles

0

0    15km

Brazilian infantry and cavalry taking the bridge over the Ytororó Stream, on December 6, 1868.

Paraguayan positions at Angostura, the Alliance forces would then transfer back to the east bank, ready to attack the Pikysyry Line from the rear.

The special task force for building the road in the Chaco was disembarked on October 11, 1868; by November 27, the works had been completed and Caxias moved to the western bank to assume command of the Alliance Army. López was taken by surprise when, in early December, 19,000 Alliance soldiers crossed the Paraguay River and appeared to the rear of his position. After landing, Caxias launched his offensive against the Pikysyry Line, which became known as the *Dezembrada*, or December Campaign. In order to move further east, the Alliance Army had to cross the Ytororó Stream; both wide and deep, this presented a serious obstacle for Caxias' forces. Initially, the only bridge crossing the river was lightly defended by the Paraguayans. On December 6, however, López sent 5,000 men with 12 guns to the area before the Alliance could begin their final advance. The ensuing Battle of Ytororó proved to be a bloody clash for both sides, with the bridge changing hands several times in attack and counterattack that witnessed brutal hand-to-hand fighting. A final, desperate charge led in person by Caxias saw the Alliance take possession of the bridge.

## THE BATTLES OF AVAY AND LOMAS VALENTINAS

On December 11, 1868, Caxias resumed the offensive, moving against 5,000 Paraguayans under General Caballero, who had entrenched themselves near the Avay Stream. Caballero's mission was to delay the Alliance advance for as long as possible, in order to permit the reorganization of the Paraguayan Army north of the Pikysyry Line; the Alliance, however, enjoyed a clear numerical advantage. After a battle lasting five hours, fought in a heavy rainstorm, the Alliance troops were able to overcome Caballero's men, having been repulsed during several earlier attempts. The Paraguayans used two elevated ridges to their advantage, but wasted many soldiers' lives in futile counterattacks. A final flanking attack by the Brazilian cavalry ended the battle, eliminating any possibility of retreat for the defeated Paraguayans. By the end of the day, Caballero's entire force had been wiped out.

The war was now entering its final phase, and both sides had no intention of giving quarter to the enemy. By now, López was ready to fight his last battle against the Alliance: he had assembled most of his remaining forces, 3,000 men, in a new fortified camp located at a site called Lomas Valentinas. The Paraguayan dictator wanted to face the Alliance in a defensive battle,

**OPPOSITE**
A map of the Battle of Avay, showing the Alliance attack against the Paraguayan defensive positions.

given that his troops were heavily outnumbered. In addition to the soldiers deployed at Lomas Valentinas, the Paraguayans had 2,000 men still defending the Pikysyry Line and 700 soldiers garrisoning the two batteries at Angostura, which were bombarded almost every day by the Brazilian fleet. On December 21, before investing López's army on the heights of Lomas Valentinas, Caxias ordered a general offensive against the Pikysyry Line: it was attacked simultaneously from the south and from the north by a total of 8,000 Alliance soldiers. The Paraguayan defensive line was quickly overwhelmed, but some 700 men were able to escape capture, with 500 making for Angostura, and 200 for Lomas Valentinas.

The Battle of Avay, by Pedro Américo, one of the most important Brazilian painters of the 19th century.

On December 21, Caxias' 18,000-strong force moved against the Paraguayan entrenched camp, for the final, decisive act of the *Dezembrada*. The Paraguayan position was protected to the front and the sides by a ditch and its excavated earth bank. The Battle of Lomas Valentinas lasted for six days, and was the last pitched battle of the Paraguayan War. During the first day, despite suffering heavy losses, the Alliance was able to take some key sections of the Paraguayan trenches. On 22 December, López received 1,600 reinforcements, but these were mostly boys aged between 12 and

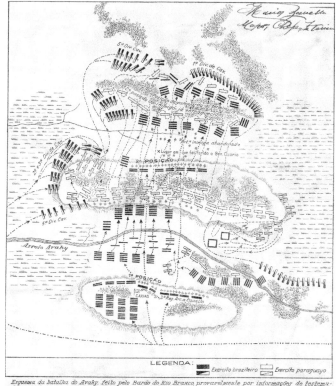

*Esquema da batalha do Avahy, feito pelo Barão do Rio Branco, provavelmente por informações de testemunhas oculares, e encontrado entre os papeis do seu arquivo.*

85

The Argentine line infantry assaulting the Paraguayan positions at the Battle of Lomas Valentinas.

14. The fighting continued during the following day with the Paraguayans showing enormous courage: each section taken by the Alliance troops cost Caxias a significant number of dead and wounded. On December 24, the Alliance commander formally requested the surrender of López, since it was by now clear that the defenders were in no condition to continue the fight for long. López refused, and the following day the Alliance bombarded the Paraguayans with all their field pieces. At the end of the 25th, Caxias had not occupied any new terrain, but the bombardment had caused great losses among the Paraguayans. On December 26, the Brazilians conducted a further bombardment, and launched several assaults, but these were all repulsed. The few remaining Paraguayans appeared to be almost indestructable. On the following day, Caxias decided to use the Argentine and Uruguayan contingents, and rest his exhausted Brazilian troops. Both the Argentines (4,800 men) and the Uruguayans (600 soldiers) showed great courage in assaulting the Paraguayan positions: supported by the Brazilian infantry, they were finally able to overcome the Paraguayan main trench and attacked Lopez's headquarters. At the end of the day, the Paraguayan camp at Lomas Valentinas had been taken; of the original 3,000 defenders, half were dead and the rest had been captured. Incredibly, López was among the few Paraguayans to escape, together with his 60-strong mounted bodyguard and a few other cavalrymen.

Caxias had crushed the remnants of the Paraguayan Army, but had missed out on capturing López, which would have brought the war to an immediate end. On December 30, running short of ammunition, the defenders at Angostura's batteries decided to surrender. On January 1, 1869, Alliance troops entered the Paraguayan capital Asunción. The *Dezembrada*, Caxias' masterpiece, was over; having captured Asunción, the great Brazilian military leader decided to resign the supreme command due to health problems.

## THE HILLS CAMPAIGN, AND THE DEATH OF LÓPEZ, 1869–70

Soon after conquering Asunción, the Brazilians formed a new, provisional Paraguayan government with collaboratist officers who had served in the Paraguayan Legion, a military unit that included several leading anti-López personalities. The war was apparently over, since López was by now a mere fugitive with a few hundred ragged followers; yet he had no intention of

Paraguayan prisoners captured during the closing phase of the war. Note the Brazilian soldiers on the balcony looking down into the courtyard filled with prisoners.

surrendering, and headed into the highlands of northeastern Paraguay to continue his hopeless fight. He intended to start a long guerrilla campaign, in which he could count on his superior knowledge of the terrain to ambush Alliance forces.

The Alliance had suffered sizable losses during the *Dezembrada* and thus was slow to dispatch forces to capture López, which gave him enough time to assemble a new, but small, army. On April 26, 1869, this period of Alliance inactivity came to an end with the arrival of the new commander-in-chief, the Brazilian Count of Eu—a young French noble, and the son-in-law of the emperor. The morale of the Brazilians at this point was low, with few, if any, wishing to continue the war: the arrival of the count, however, led to a reorganization of Alliance military forces for a rapid campaign to capture López. The latter had been able to assemble his force by uniting the soldiers from Asunción's garrison (who had abandoned the city before the arrival of the Alliance) together with several thousand formerly wounded veterans, and with several hundred volunteer Amerindians. His force totaled 9,000 men and possessed 40 field guns of differing calibers.

López did not have enough men to attack the Brazilians on a large scale, and thus launched a series of small raids that caused minor Alliance losses. The main objective of these incursions was to capture weapons and horses, since his men were mostly armed with pikes. López's guerrillas also targeted railroad and telegraph lines.

On May 18, 1869, the Count of Eu moved to the offensive, with the intention of finding the Paraguayan dictator as soon as possible. Despite their great numerical superiority, the Brazilians had serious difficulties in taking control of the towns and villages that were still under López's control: the small Paraguayan garrisons defending them routinely did their best to resist. On August 12, the Alliance attacked the town of Piribebuy, located in a solid defensive position surrounded by hills and which had a garrison of 1,600 soldiers armed with 12 artillery pieces. After a heavy bombardment, the Brazilians assaulted Piribebuy with their infantry from

Paraguayan civilian refugees from the city of San Pedro, with a Brazilian priest. This photograph was probably taken in the hospital of the Brazilian Navy in Asunción, during late May 1869.

three sides, and then used their cavalry to clear through the streets of the town. At the conclusion of the fighting, all the Paraguayan defenders had been killed or captured.

With the Alliance now hot on his heels, López decided to detach his best remaining units from the main body of his force to form a rearguard under the command of General Caballero. This force, mostly formed of aging veterans and boys, was tasked with intercepting the advancing Alliance troops in order to delay them. It consisted of 3,600 men and 12 guns. The Paraguayans awaited the Alliance troops in a defensive position on the broken terrain of Acosta Ñu/Campo Grande: the ensuing battle saw Caballero and his men wiped out, with all men killed or captured, as at Piribebuy. August 16, the day of the Battle of Acosta Ñu/Campo Grande, is still remembered today in Paraguay as the "Day of the Children" due to the high number of boys who died in this clash.

After the defeats at Piribebuy and Acosta Ñu, the few remaining Paraguayans had little choice but to retreat further north, avoiding contact with the Alliance. By December 1869, after several more months

Brazilian cavalry officers, wearing their dark blue campaign uniforms and kepis. On the right, standing next to the trumpeter, is the corporal known as "Chico Diablo," who killed Francisco Solano López at Cerro Corá.

of skirmishing and retreating, López had just 4,000 followers left; over the following weeks, most died from starvation, or deserted, reducing the number down to a few hundred. On March 1, 1870, the Brazilians were finally able to surprise the last Paraguayans in their final encampment at Cerro Corá. During the ensuing battle, the 500 Paraguayans were wiped out by the Brazilians, who encircled the whole Cerro Corá valley before launching their attack. Francisco Solano López was killed fighting with his sword in hand, shouting "¡Muero con mi Pátria!" ("I die with my Homeland!") The Paraguayan War was over.

# AFTERMATH

The Paraguayan War had a profound impact on the destinies of all four countries involved in the conflict, but for Paraguay in particular it marked a major turning point. The defeated country lost 54,000 square miles of its territory to Brazil and Argentina, almost half of its prewar extent. In addition, the rest of Paraguay's territory was occupied by Alliance troops until 1876. Under the joint occupation, tension between Brazil and Argentina threatened to spark into a new armed conflict. Initially, the Argentine negotiators proposed dividing Paraguay up between Argentina and Brazil, but the Brazilians refused, preferring to maintain a buffer state between themselves and their old rival.

From 1870 until the end of the century, Paraguay experienced a chronic economic and social crisis, since only some 28,000 of its 160,000-odd surviving inhabitants were adult males. Postwar Paraguay had a female:male

A photo showing soldiers from the Paraguayan Legion and the Uruguayan Voluntários de la Libertad infantry battalion (the latter on the right, in the background). Militarily unimportant, the Paraguayan Legion comprised a certain number of emigré anti-López Paraguayans, many of whom would become members of the new Paraguayan government installed by the Brazilians after capturing Asunción in 1869.

# Paraguay after the war

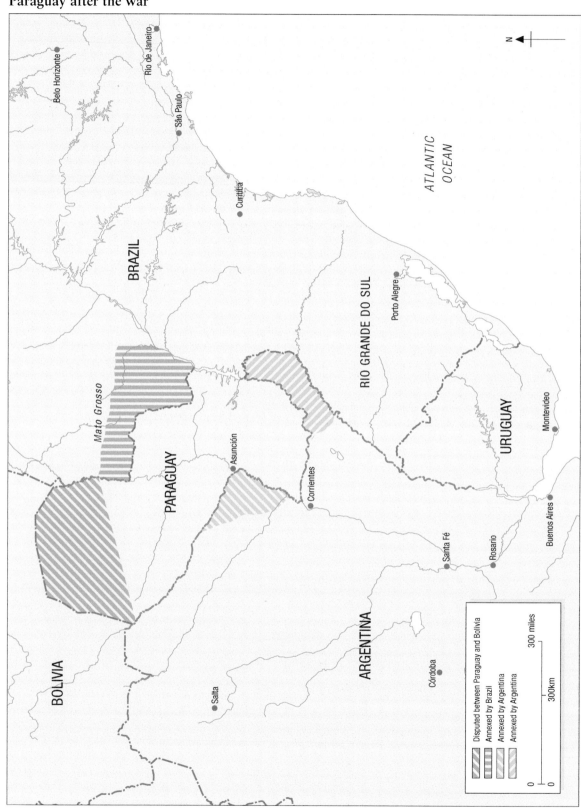

**Legend:**
- Disputed between Paraguay and Bolivia
- Annexed by Brazil
- Annexed by Argentina
- Annexed by Argentina

BRAZIL

BOLIVIA

PARAGUAY

ARGENTINA

URUGUAY

RIO GRANDE DO SUL

Mato Grosso

ATLANTIC OCEAN

Belo Horizonte

Rio de Janeiro

São Paulo

Curitiba

Porto Alegre

Montevideo

Asunción

Corrientes

Santa Fé

Rosario

Buenos Aires

Córdoba

Salta

N

0 — 300 miles
0 — 300km

imbalance of at least 4:1, which increased to 20:1 in the most devastated areas. The war helped Brazil reach a peak of political and military influence in South America, becoming the major power in the continent. It also was the principle factor that led to the end of slavery in the empire; thousands of black volunteers had taken part in the conflict in hopes of obtaining liberty and greater personal freedoms.

After 1870, the military acquired a key role in the Brazilian public sphere, starting a trend that would continue to the present. However, the Paraguayan War also caused a ruinous increase in the public debt, which took decades to pay off, severely limiting Brazil's economic growth. The war debt, coupled with an enduring social crisis, is considered to be one of the crucial factors in the fall of the empire in 1889 and the proclamation of the First Brazilian Republic.

After the war, Argentina faced several Federalist revolts against the central government. However, the conflict had played a key role in consolidating Argentina into a unified nation (fighting against a common enemy) and all the rebellions that followed the war were put down by the central government. By the end of the century, Argentina was the most prosperous nation in South America, enjoying wide-ranging overseas trade and possessing a large fleet.

Victory in the War of the Triple Alliance permitted the liberal *Colorados* in Uruguay to retain control over the state until as late as 1958, defeating all the subsequent revolts of the *Blancos*. After this devastating continental war, South-American armies were never the same: the need for professionalism increased greatly, as did continuous research into new military technologies. The era of the gaucho army had come to an end in the La Plata basin: modern warfare had demonstrated its full potential during the 1864–70 conflict, and revealed the limitations of previous military models.

# THE BATTLEFIELD TODAY

The Paraguayan War is still remembered today in Paraguay as the most important and heroic episode in national history, together with the Chaco War of 1932–35 fought against Bolivia. Despite this, however, there are only a few museums specifically dedicated to the great conflict of 1864–70. Out of these, the best and probably most significant are the Museo Paso de Patria, and the Museo del ex-Cuartel de Mariscal López. Both contain a large amount of archaeological finds dating back to the time of the war, mostly weapons or pieces of equipment that were found over the decades during local excavations. These objects are extremely precious for understanding the material culture of the soldiers involved in the war, and are invaluable for any historian interested in the study of this conflict. Both institutions are near some of the most important battlefield sites described in this book, which were all fought in quite a small area. The Museo Paso de Patria is close to Tuyutí and Curupaytí, while the Museo del ex-Cuartel de Mariscal López is at Humaitá. Guides at both museums are available for excursions at the three main sites.

This simple monument, located on the battlefield of Tuyutí, commemorates the Paraguayan soldiers who lost their lives between 1864 and 1870. (Courtesy of Vicente Garcia and Vicenta Miranda Ojeda, Museo Paso de Patria and Museo del ex-Cuartel de Mariscal López; author's collection)

Today, the battlefield of Tuyutí looks exactly as it did in 1866, save for a few simple Paraguayan monuments erected on it. The same can be said for the battlefield of Curupaytí, where the remnants of the Paraguayan trenches can still partly be seen and explored. Nothing remains, though, of Humaitá: destroying this fortress was one of the main common objectives that led to the birth of the Triple Alliance, and today nothing is visible of the original structures. The only exception comprises the remains of Humaitá church, which was part of the complex built around the fortress.

The two museums are relatively easy to reach from the Paraguayan capital of Asunción, located 270 miles north of Humaitá: travelling on Ruta 4 (Highway 4) by car or bus brings you to Pilar, which is just 25 miles from Humaitá. Once at Pilar, take Ruta 6 (Highway 6) for Humaitá itself. At the Museo del ex-Cuartel de Mariscal López, local guides can escort visitors to the sites of Tuyutí and Curupaytí, which are located just a few miles to the south. In addition to the above sites, anyone interested in the

The museum of Paso de Patria, the main cultural institution of Paraguay that preserves the memory of the great conflict fought between 1864 and 1870. (Courtesy of Vicente Garcia and Vicenta Miranda Ojeda, Museo Paso de Patria and Museo del ex-Cuartel de Mariscal López; author's collection)

Paraguayan War should also visit the official museum of the Paraguayan Army. The Instituto de Historia y Museo Militar is located in the center of Asunción and is well worth a visit. It has an entire room dedicated to Francisco Solano López, and another full of original weapons dating back to the Paraguayan War.

A monument dedicated to Francisco Solano López, bearing his famous motto "Victory or Death," located near the museum of Paso de Patria, Paraguay. (Courtesy of Vicente Garcia and Vicenta Miranda Ojeda, Museo Paso de Patria and Museo del ex-Cuartel de Mariscal López; author's collection)

# BIBLIOGRAPHY AND FURTHER READING

### The war

Abente, D., "The War of the Triple Alliance: Three Explanatory Models," in *Latin American Research Review*, 22/2, Miami, 1987

Box, P. H., *The Origins of the Paraguayan War*, Russel & Russel, New York, 1967

Chiavenato, J. J., *Genocídio Americano: A Guerra do Paraguai*, Brasiliense, São Paulo, 1979

Doratioto, F., *Maldita Guerra: Nueva Historia de la Guerra del Paraguay*, Emecé, Buenos Aires, 2008

Fragoso, A. T., *História da Guerra entre a Tríplice Aliança e o Paraguai*, Rio de Janeiro, 1934

Herken Krauer, J. C., and Giménez de Herken, M. I., *Gran Bretaña y la Guerra de la Triple Alianza*, Arte Nuevo, Asunción, 1983

Kolinski, C. J., *Independence or Death! The Story of the Paraguayan War*, University of Florida Press, Gainesville, 1965

Kraay, H., and Whigham, T. L., *I Die with My Country: Perspectives on the Paraguayan War, 1864–1870*, Thomson-Shore, Dexter, 2004

Lynch, J., "The River Plate Republics from Independence to the Paraguayan War," in *The Cambridge History of Latin America*, Vol. 3, Cambridge, 1985

McLynn, F. J., "The Causes of the War of the Triple Alliance: An Interpretation," in *Inter-American Economic Affairs*, 33/2, Washington, 1979–80

——, "Consequences for Argentina of the War of the Triple Alliance 1865–70," in *The Americas*, 41/1, Cambridge, 1984–85

Plá, J., *The British in Paraguay, 1850–1870*, Richmond Publishing Company, Richmond, 1976

Reber, V. B., "The Demographics of Paraguay: A Reinterpretation of the Great War, 1864–70," in *Hispanic American Historical Review*, 68/2, Durham, 1988

Salles, R., *Guerra do Paraguai: Escravidão e Cidadania na Formação do Exército*, Paz e Terra, Rio de Janeiro, 2008

Soares, Á. T., *O Drama da Tríplice Aliança: 1865–1876*, Brand, Rio de Janeiro, 1956

Sodré, N. W., *História Militar do Brasil*, Expressão Popular, São Paulo, 1965

Tate, E. N., "Britain and Latin America in the 19th century: The Case of Paraguay, 1811–1870," in *Ibero-Amerikanisches Institut Archiv*, 5/1, Frankfurt, 1979

Whigham, T. L., *The Politics of River Trade: Tradition and Development in the Upper Plata, 1780–1870*, University of New Mexico Press, Albuquerque, 1991

Williams, J. H., *The Rise and Fall of the Paraguayan Republic, 1800–1870*, Institute of Latin American Studies, Austin, 1979

### The armies

Duarte, Paulo de Queiroz, *Os Voluntários da Pátria na Guerra do Paraguai*, Bibliex, Rio de Janeiro, 1981–84

Esposito, G., *The War of the Triple Alliance*, Winged Hussar Publishing, Point Pleasant, 2017

Hooker, T. D., *Armies of the 19th Century: The Americas—The Paraguayan War*, Foundry Books, Nottingham, 2008

Luqui-Lagleyze, J. M., *Los Cuerpos Militares en la Historia Argentina: Organización y Uniformes 1550–1950*, Instituto Nacional Sanmartiniano, Buenos Aires, 1995

Rodrigues, J. W., and Barroso, G., *Uniformes do Exército Brasileiro, 1730–1922*, Rio de Janeiro, 1922

Udaondo, E., *Uniformes Militares Usados en la Argentina Desde el Siglo XVI hasta Nuestros Días*, Buenos Aires, 1922

# INDEX

Figures in bold refer to illustrations.

Acosta Ñu/Campo Grande, Battle of 88
*Amazonas* (Brazilian frigate) 33, **33**, 44
American Civil War 4
Angostura 35, 84, 86
Argentina 4, 8, 11, 12–14, 34–35, 35, 48, 89, 91
Argentine Army
   *3 de Oro* (Golden Three) 30
   artillery 29, 30, **30**, 31
   cavalry 29, 30, **30**, 31
   commanders 23–24, **23**
   demobilized 35
   engineers 29
   gauchos **36**
   General Lavalle Cavalry Regiment 30
   General San Martín Cavalry Regiment 30
   infantry 29, **29**, 30, 31, **31**, 68–70
   Legión Militar **14**
   Legions of Volunteers **13**, 29
   National Guard 29, 30, 31, **31**, 35, 49
   organization 29
   San Nicolás Battalion 30
   staff officer **30**
   strength 29, 29–30
   weapons 31
   *zapadores* 29
Arroyo Grande, Battle of 14
Asunción 81, 86
Avay, Battle of 84, **85**

balloons 76
Barreto, João de Deus Mena 36
Barrios, José Vicente **20**, 21, 37, 57, **58–60**, 61
Belgrano, Manuel 6, 8
*Belmonte* (Brazilian ship) 44
Berro, Bernardo 12
Boquerón del Sauce, Battle of 65–67, **65**, **66**
Brazil 4, 10–12, 13, 15, 34, 48
   intervention in Uruguay 36–37
   Maranhão province 21–22
   objective 35
   postwar 89, 91
   Uruguayan War intervention 15, **15**
Brazilian Army 24, 34
   1st Division 36
   2nd Division 36
   16º Corpo de Voluntários Auxiliar 12
   artillery 27, 28, 29
   assault on Paysandú 37
   Balloon Corps 76
   *Caçadores* battalions 28
   cavalry 27, 28, 28–29, **29**, 50, **58–60**, 88

commanders 21–23, **21**, **22**
Corpo de Voluntários da Pátria **27**, 28, **29**, 40, 49, 76, 78
Duke of Caxias appointed commander 76, 78
engineers 28
First Battle of Tuyutí **58–60**, 61
*Guardias Nacionales* 27
infantry 27, **27**, 28
organization 27–28
reorganization 78
sappers **28**
strength 27, 28
Train Squadron 28
volunteers 28, 76
weapons 28–29, **58–60**
Zuavos da Bahia **11**
Brazilian Navy 33, **33**, 35, 40, 50–51, 66, 67, 78, 80–1, 82
   Battle of Curupaytí 71
   Battle of the Riachuelo 41, 44–45, **44**
Buenos Aires 13, 23, 30

Caballero, Bernardino 21, 88
campaign
   1868–69 83 (map)
   advance on Paraguay 46, 47 (map), 48–51
   assault on Paysandú 37
   Battle of Acosta Ñu/Campo Grande 88
   Battle of Avay 84, **85**
   Battle of Boquerón del Sauce 65–67, **65**, **66**
   Battle of Cerro Corá 88
   Battle of Curupaytí 67, 68–70, 71–73, **71**, **73**, **74–75** (map)
   Battle of Curuzú 67
   Battle of Estero Bellaco 51, **52–54**, 55
   Battle of Itapirú 50–51
   Battle of Lomas Valentinas 84–86, **86**
   Battle of Paso de Patria 49
   Battle of São Borja 40–41, **40**
   Battle of the Riachuelo 4, 35, **38**, 41, **41**, **42–43** (map), 44–45, **44**
   Battle of Yatay 45, **45**
   Battle of Yataytí Corá 66
   Battle of Ytororó 84, **84**
   Brazilian intervention in Uruguay 36–37
   the *Dezembrada* 84–86, 87
   fall of Humaitá 79–82, **81**
   First Battle of Tuyutí 4, **20**, 55–57, **57**, 57, **58–60**, 61, **61**, **62–63** (map), 64–65, **64**
   Hills Campaign 86–88
   invasion of Misiones province 40–41
   invasion of Paraguay 77 (map), 78

invasion of Río Grande do Sul 38, **39** (map)
long stalemate 76, 78
occupation of Corrientes 38, **38**, 40
opening of hostilities 36–37
origins of 4–6
Pikysyry Line Offensive 85
the Pikysyry Maneuver 82, 84
Second Battle of Tuyutí 78–79, **80**
Siege of Uruguayana 45–46, **46**
Caseros, Battle of 13, 23, **24**
Caxias, Duke of **10**, 21–22, **21**, 76, 78, 79, 84, 85, 86
Cepeda, Battle of 13–14, 23
Cerro Corá, Battle of 88
Cetz, Colonel Juan Fernando 29
Chaco, the 9, 78
*chatas* 33, 41, 44, 50
chronology 16–18
Cisplatine War 13, 24
climate 6
Corrientes 47 (map), 48
   occupation of 38, **38**, 40
*Cruzada Libertadora* 15, 24, 36
Cuiabá 37
Curupaytí 48, 65, 78, 82
Curupaytí, Battle of **74–75** (map), 76, 92
   Alliance attack **68–70**, 73
   Alliance retreat 73
   casualties 73
   defenses 67, 71, **71**, **73**
   forces 72
   naval bombardment 71, 73
   order of battle 72
Curuzú 48, 65, 66, 67

Day of the Children, the 88
*Dezembrada*, the 84–86, 87

El Criollo 35
Establecimiento 80
Estero Bellaco, Battle of 51, **52–54**, 55
Estigarribia, José Félix 40–41, 45, 45–46
Eu, Count of **10**, 22–23, **22**, 87

*Farrapos* Revolt 9, 12
Flores, Venancio 12, 15, **19**, 24, 32, 36, 37, 51, 61, 71, 76
France 14, 76
Francia, José Gaspar Rodriguez de 8

Garibaldi, Giuseppe 14
Great Britain 76
*Gualeguay* (Paraguayan ship) 50

Hills Campaign 86–88
Humaitá, Fortress of 5, 9, 35, 48, 76, 78, 80, 92

evacuation of 82
fall of 79–82, **81**

Itapirú, Battle of 50–51
Itatí 49

*Jejui* (Paraguayan ship) 44
*Jequitinhonha* (Brazilian ship) 44

Lavalle, Juan 13
Lisboa, Joaquim Marques Lisboa,
    Marquis of Tamandaré 73
Lomas Valentinas, Battle of 84–86, **86**
López, Carlos António 8–9
López, Francisco Solano 9, 12, 19–20,
    **19**, **20**, 21, 25, 26, 35, 36, 36–37,
    37, 48, 71
    Battle of Boquerón del Sauce 65–67
    Battle of Curupaytí 67, 71
    Battle of Estero Bellaco 51, **52–54**
    Battle of Itapirú 51
    Battle of Lomas Valentinas 84–85,
        85–86, **86**
    Battle of Paso de Patria 49
    Battle of the Riachuelo 41
    death of 88
    the *Dezembrada* 84
    fall of Humaitá 81
    First Battle of Tuyutí 57, **58–60**, 61
    Hills Campaign 86–88
    invasion of Misiones province 40–41
    invasion of Río Grande do Sul 38
    mistakes 34–35
    monument **93**
    objective 82
    orders defense of Paraguayan
        national territory 46
    Pikysyry headquarters 82
    plans 34–35
    Second Battle of Tuyutí 78
    Yataytí Corá peace talks 71

*Marquês de Olinda* (Brazilian ship) 36
Mato Grosso 9–10, 34, 37
Mexico 4
Meza, Pedro Ignacio 41, 44
military experts 6
Misiones province 40–41, 48
Mitre, Bartolomé 14, **19**, 23–24, 24,
    29, 29–30, 34–35, 35, 38, 46, 48,
    49, 61, **71**, 73, 76, 78
Montevideo 14, 23, 37
    Great Siege of 14–15, 24
Montevideo, Treaty of 11
monuments 92, **92**, **93**
museums 92, 92–93, **93**

Napoleon III, Emperor 20
Nueva Coimbra 37

Oribe, Manuel 14–15
Osório, Manuel Luís 50

Pallejas, León de 24, **65**
*Paraguarí* (Paraguayan corvette) 33
Paraguay 4, 6, **7** (map), 8–10, 12, 15
    Blancos 37
    defensive system **48**
    invasion of **77** (map), 78
    plans 34–35
    postwar 89, **90** (map), 91
Paraguay River 9, 33, 36, **48**, 65, 67,
    71, 78, 80
Paraguayan Army 8
    Acá Carayá 26
    Acá Verá 26
    artillery 25, 26, 26–27, **35**
    cavalry 25, 26, **26**, 58–60
    commanders 19–21, **19**, **20**
    infantry 25, 25–26, **25**, **26**, 50,
        **52–54**, 68–70
    organization 25–26
    raids 49–50
    strength 25–26
    weapons 26–27, **52–54**, **58–60**, 68–70
Paraguayan Legion 89
Paraguayan Navy 9, 33, 38, 46, 50,
    81, 82
    Battle of the Riachuelo 41, 44–45
Paraná River 9, 33, **35**, 41, **44**, 48,
    50–51
Paso de la Patria 48, 50, 51, 55
Paso de Patria, Battle of 48–49
Paunero, Wenceslao 24, 40
Pavón, Battle of 14
Paysandú **15**, 37
Paz, General José María 8
Pedro I, Emperor of Brazil 11–12, 21
Pedro II, Emperor of Brazil **10**, 12,
    21–22, 46, **46**, 48
Pikysyry **82**
Pikysyry Line Offensive 85
Piribebuy 87–88
Portugal 10, 11–12
prisoners of war 55, 81, 87

refugees **88**
Riachuelo, Battle of the 4, 35, **38**, 41,
    **41**, **42–43** (map), 44–45, **44**
Río de Janeiro 12, 21
*Río de Janeiro* (Brazilian ironclad) 66
Río Grande do Sul 9–10, 12, 34, 37,
    **39** (map), 45, 46, **47** (map)
River Plate/Río de la Plata 9, 11, 12,
    13, 36
Rivera, José Fructuoso 14–15, 24
Robles, Wenceslao 38
rocket-launchers 27, 49
Rosas, Juan Manuel de 8, 9, 12, 13,
    14–15, 23

San Borja, Battle of 40–41, **40**
Saxe-Coburg-Gotha, Duke of **10**
Spain 10, 12
stirrups **76**

*Tacuarí* (Paraguayan corvette) 33
Tayí 80
Triple Alliance, the 4
    commanders **10**, 21–24, **21**, **22**, **23**
    differences in opinion 76
    forces 27–32, 55
    invasion of Paraguay **77** (map), 78
    long stalemate 76, 78
    plans 35, 78
    supply shortage 65
Triple Alliance, Treaty of the 38
Tuyutí **48**, 76, 92, **92**
Tuyutí, First Battle of 4, 20, 55, **61**, 64
    Alliance victory 64–65
    Brazilian cavalry counterattack
        58–60, **61**
    casualties 58–60, 64
    dispositions 57, **58–60**
    order of battle 55–57
    Paraguayan advance **61**, 64
Tuyutí, Second Battle of 78–79, **79**

United States of America 76
Urquiza, Justo José de 12, 15–16, 23,
    **23**, 34, 35, 48
Uruguay 4, 10–11, 12, 13, 14–15, 24
    *Blancos* 14–15, 24, 34, 36, 48, 76
    Brazilian intervention 36–37
    objective 35
    postwar 91
Uruguay River 9, 40–41, 46
Uruguayan Army 32, 45
    *24 de Abril* **52–54**, 57
    artillery 66
    commanders 24
    *División Oriental* (Oriental Division)
        32
    Florida Battalion 24
    infantry **52–54**
    Vanguard Division 49
    Voluntários da Pátria **45**
    Voluntários de la Libertad 89
    weapons 32
Uruguayan Navy 33
Uruguayan War 15, **15**
Uruguayana, Siege of 45–46, **46**

Velasco, Bernardo de 6, 8
Vuelta de Humaitá 80

waterways 32–33

Yatay, Battle of 45, **45**
Yataytí Corá, Battle of 66
Yataytí Corá peace talks 71, **71**
Ytororó, Battle of 84, **84**